UNEXPLAINED
SOUTH

The **UNDERWATER FOREST** of **ALABAMA**
INEXPLICABLE LIGHTS over **TEXAS**,
The **RED-EYED MONSTER** of **ARKANSAS**
& MORE RICH SOUTHERN MYSTERY

ALAN BROWN

Published by The History Press
Charleston, SC
www.historypress.com

Front cover: Illustrations by Sarah Haynes.
Back cover, inset: The "Drummer Boy of Shiloh," John Clem. *Heritage Auctions*; *back cover, bottom*: The baptism of Virginia Dare, the first English child born in the New World. *William A. Crafts*.

First published 2019

Manufactured in the United States

ISBN 9781467142380

Library of Congress Control Number: 2019948663

CONTENTS

CONTENTS

Contents

CONTENTS

INTRODUCTION

A legend is a regional oral narrative, usually based in fact. Over time, through various retellings, the facts become so distorted that it is often difficult to separate the truth from fiction. The American Southeast is one of the most legendary parts of the country. In fact, one could say that the South is a fertile breeding ground for oral history, folklore and legends. Anyone who has visited the South knows that southerners love to talk, especially about the history and lore of their community. Owing to the region's long history, southerners have a wealth of material to draw on. Indeed, southern legends are populated by Native Americans, Spanish explorers, British colonists, witches, pirates, Civil War soldiers, slaves, outlaws and bank robbers. Legends provide people with the means through which they can preserve the history of their town or city, made unique by the personal elements contributed by the storytellers.

Legends perform other functions as well. In the preface to *More Great Southern Mysteries* (1990), author E. Randall Floyd says that early legends reflect humans' attempt to make sense of things that they do not understand: "They go back to a time perhaps when every creaking thing in nature had its own sinister purpose—the sun, the rain, the wind, the moon, the shadows, the forest." Some of the stories in this work that seem to serve this purpose are "The Devil's Hoofprints" (Bath, North Carolina), "The Face in the Courthouse Window" (Carrollton, Alabama) and "John Rowan's Restless Tombstone" (Bardstown, Kentucky). Other legends are intriguing because they challenge our views of nature, such as "The Kentucky Meat

Shower" (Bath, Kentucky) and "The Crying Pecan Tree of Choctaw County" (Needham, Alabama). Strange disappearances, such as "What Really Happened to Theodosia Burr?" (Nags Head, North Carolina) or "Roanoke, The Lost Colony" (Dare County, North Carolina), stimulate our imaginations as we entertain different theories concerning their fate. Legends dealing with UFOs (for example, "The Aurora Incident" from Aurora, Texas, and "The Pascagoula Alien Abduction" from Pascagoula, Mississippi) suggest that our accepted view of the earth and its place in the universe might need to be revised. Some legends suggest that history might need to be rewritten entirely ("John St. Helen's True Identity" from Granbury, Texas, and "Virginia's Jack the Ripper" from Norfolk, Virginia). Urban legends, such as "Three-Legged Lady Road" (Columbus, Mississippi), are instructive in that they reflect contemporary fears, like the fear of driving out to out-of-the-way places at night.

Jan Harold Brunvand (*The Vanishing Hitchhiker: American Urban Legends & Their Meanings*) says that most legends cannot be taken as literal accounts of events because of their narrative structure, their oral variations and their traditional motifs. Rejecting legends for this reason alone ignores what is possibly their most important reason for existence: their entertainment value. Everyone is fascinated by the unknown, the uncanny. Even more importantly, legends suggest that there might be another dimension to reality that surfaces only in these strange little stories that stimulate our imagination. How boring would life be without fantastic, but supposedly true, stories like "The Marfa Lights" (Marfa, Texas), "The Fouke Monster" (Fouke, Arkansas) and "The Treasure of Hampton Plantation" (Charleston, South Carolina)?

1

UNEARTHLY IMAGES

ALBERT RUSSEL ERSKINE'S MAUSOLEUM

Huntsville, Alabama

Albert Russel Erskine was born in Huntsville, Alabama, on January 24, 1871. He attended the state's public schools. When he was fifteen, he was hired as an office boy for fifteen dollars per month in a Huntsville railroad office. Eventually, he moved up to the position of chief bookkeeper. After moving to St. Louis, Erskine was hired by the American Cotton Company. Soon, he became chief clerk and, in a short while, was appointed general auditor and manager of operations of over three hundred cotton gins. He became a CPA (certified public accountant) in 1908. Between 1905 and 1920, he served as treasurer and member of the board of Yale & Towne Manufacturing Company and as a vice president and member of the board of directors for the Underwood Typewriter Company.

In 1911, Erskine joined the Studebaker Company in South Bend, Indiana. Studebaker began producing electric automobiles in 1902. Its first gas-powered car rolled off the lines in 1914. After Erskine became president of the company in 1915, Studebaker purchased the luxury automaker Pierce-Arrow. The company began producing the affordably priced Erskine and Rockne models in the 1920s, but the cars never caught on with the general public. Studebaker suffered severe financial setbacks in the early 1930s. Erskine was accused of mismanagement, even though many companies were being hit hard during the Great Depression. In March 1933, Studebaker filed for bankruptcy. Erskine killed himself on July 1, 1933.

Albert Russel Erskine was interred in an ornate mausoleum in Huntsville's Maple Hill Cemetery. For years, visitors to the cemetery claimed to have seen the figure of an angel on the door. However, the "angel" was probably produced by oxidation on the door's metallic surface.

THE DEVIL'S HOOFPRINTS

Bath, North Carolina

One of North Carolina's most enduring legends is set in Bath, North Carolina, in the early 1800s. The protagonist of the tale is a handsome young scoundrel named Jesse Elliot, who had a reputation as the owner of the fastest horse in the area. He cashed in on his reputation by racing his horse against all comers on Sunday afternoons. Invariably, Elliot's horse won, earning his master a great deal of money.

Elliot's winning streak came to an abrupt end one Sunday in 1802 when he was approached at the docks by a dark stranger. The man asked Elliot if he thought his horse was the fastest in the entire county. Elliot raised his head haughtily and answered, "Yes, I am sure he can beat any horse around here." Smiling, the stranger wagered $100 that his horse could outrun Elliot's in a fair race. The pair agreed to meet at the racetrack in an hour.

As Elliot rode his horse home to ready for the race, he was filled with misgivings. There was something about the stranger's appearance and manner that was unsettling. At home, he gulped down two large glasses of whiskey to bolster his courage and informed his wife that he was going to a horse race. His wife, who tired of her husband's blasphemous behavior, told him that he was pressing his luck by racing on Sunday. Pulling on his racing boots, Elliot cursed his wife for a fool. As he strode out the door, she shouted angrily, "I hope you'll be sent to hell this very day."

Riding up to the gate of the racetrack, Elliot could see the dark stranger holding the reins of a large black steed, waiting for him. After exchanging greetings, the two men rode up to the starting post and waited for the race to begin. The starting shot was fired, and the horsemen galloped down the lane. After a minute or so, Elliot looked back over his shoulder. When he noticed that the dark stranger had fallen several lengths behind him, Elliot exclaimed, "Take me in a winner, or take me to hell!" All at once, Elliot's horse stopped dead in its tracks, catapulting Elliot over the horse's head. Elliot's body was smashed against a large pine tree. As Elliot's horse galloped away, one of his cronies ran up to his friend to see if there was something he could do to help, but Elliot was already dead.

Jesse Elliot's death had a profound effect on the community. A search was conducted for Elliot's horse, but he was never found. The next week, the town council banned horseracing. A few weeks later, one of the townspeople returned to the racetrack and examined the pine tree. He was stunned to see that the side Elliot's body had struck was dead, but the rest of the tree was green and healthy. Walking around the tree, he noticed four deep hoofprints that had not been there before. The hoofprints are still clearly visible today. Locals say that if leaves or twigs are blown into the hoofprints during the day, they will be gone the next morning. Some scientists assert that the strange depressions were produced by salt veins. Others say they may be vents for subterranean rives. However, people of a more superstitious bent believe that the hoofprints stand as proof that Jesse Elliot sent himself to hell on that fateful day back in 1802.

DANIEL KEITH'S SHADOW

Cliffside, North Carolina

Daniel Keith enjoyed a happy childhood until his father died in 1861. His mother became the sole support of the family, sewing and taking in laundry to help make ends meet. Young Daniel became angry at the world, embittered because his life had changed so drastically. The next year, fourteen-year-old Daniel Keith left home, determined to make a good life for himself. He enlisted in the Confederate army but soon found a highly regimented life not to his liking, so he went AWOL. To survive, he had to shovel out stables and perform other dirty jobs. Before long, Keith realized that he could make a good living by relying on his wits. Standing six feet, four inches and bulging with muscle, the handsome young man with blazing red hair and broad shoulders learned how to charm people out of their money, especially women. Also, he was not above "borrowing" whatever was not locked up or nailed down. Toward the end of the Civil War, Keith enlisted once again in the Confederate army, went AWOL and talked his way out of being punished.

Daniel Keith lived many years in Tennessee. In 1878, he moved to Rutherford, Tennessee, where people were looking for a lost cache of gold. Always on the watch for a new hustle, Keith decided to cash in on the people's gold fever by "creating" his own gold mine. In 1879, he rubbed down a sixty-pound rock with brass and went around Rutherford announcing that he had struck gold. Keith sold his mine to a number of gullible people until he had turned a large percentage of Rutherford against him.

His swindle was still on the minds of the people of Rutherford when the body of ten-year-old Alice Ellis was found in January 1880. She had been raped and murdered. A boy told Sheriff Walker that he had seen a large man wandering around the murder scene. His shirt and pants seemed to be soaked with blood. Another witness said that he had seen Daniel Keith staggering around the little girl's neighborhood, angry and drunk. The sheriff immediately made his way to Keith's cabin. When he walked inside, Sheriff Walker noticed immediately that Keith was calm and sober. Keith said that he had heard about the child's murder. He admitted that he had been in the area at the time of the murder but had not seen anything out of the ordinary. When Keith finished talking, the sheriff asked him about bloodstains on his shirt, which had turned brown. Keith explained that he had been skinning rabbits and did not have time to clean up. Even though Keith produced the rabbit skins and skinned rabbits, Sheriff Walker decided to arrest him for murder anyway and escorted him to the Rutherford County Jail.

In the weeks that followed, Keith angrily proclaimed his innocence, both inside the jail and out the jail window. A few months after being arrested, Keith was transferred to the Cleveland County Jail in Shelby to await trial later in the year. Predictably, the crowd sitting in the courtroom had already convicted Daniel Keith in their own minds. He had already been proven to be a liar and a thief; in fact, many of the people who sat in judgment of him had been victims of his scams. They even believed the testimony of a sixteen-year-old boy who said that he had seen Keith walking around the crime scene covered in blood, but the witness could not remember the color of the shirt. Finally, Keith took the stand. His temper flaring, he announced that he was innocent and that he would curse the entire town if he was hanged: "Each of you will be hainted every day." An hour later, Keith was found guilty of the crimes of rape and murder.

During his sentencing, Keith proclaimed that anyone who thought he was guilty would pay the devil every day.

On the day of Keith's execution, the cage in which he was shackled was transported to the gallows in a wagon, along with his coffin. The hangman placed the noose around Keith's neck. Before he covered Keith's head with a black bag, he asked the prisoner if he had any last words. In a quavering voice, Keith said, "The soul of an innocent man don't rest." He then turned to Sheriff Walker and told him to "keep cool." Keith resumed his stony gaze at the crowd and awaited the springing of the trap door. Within a few minutes, his neck was broken, and he was dangling from the gallows.

For most criminals, this would be the end of their story. Daniel Keith's legend, however, had just begun. Not long after Keith's execution, the shadowy image of a hanging man appeared on the south wall of the jail. The sheriff ordered the jailer to paint over the image, but it returned a few days later. Over time, the ghostly image resisted all attempts to cover it up with paint and whitewash. Word of the ineradicable image spread throughout the South. For years, hundreds of tourists flocked to the town to view the south wall of the jail. In 1949, the building was converted into office space. The new owners pulled down the ivy that had been growing on the south wall, fully expecting to find the image of Daniel Keith underneath. Interestingly enough, the image was gone. Around the same time, an eighty-four-year-old man who had testified against Daniel Keith at the age of sixteen died in a nursing home. Some people believed that the disappearance of the image and the death of the witness who had helped convict Keith were more than just a coincidence.

THE FACE ON THE WALL OF EWING HALL

Galveston, Texas

The University of Texas Medical Branch was founded in 1891. Today, it has grown from only one building—the Ashbel Smith Building—to more than seventy buildings. One of these buildings is Ewing Hall, which is also known as Building 71. Ewing Hall is the site of the University of Texas Medical Branch Heliport and the Department of Preventive Medicine and Community Health. It is also known for the spectral image of an old man on the waterfront side of the building.

The "ghost face" on the wall of the University of Texas Medical Branch's Ewing Hall is said to be the image of the property's original owner, whose family sold it to UTMB against his wishes. *Alan Brown*.

Two legends have been generated to explain the sudden appearance of the "ghost face." According to the best-known variant, the land on which Ewing Hall now stands was originally owned by an elderly farmer who refused to sell his property to UTMB. Just before he died, his family promised him that they would never sell the land, However, not long after the old man's death, his family ignored his last wishes and sold the property to UTMB instead of passing it down to future generations.

In the second version of the tale, the old farmer has been replaced by a historical personage named William "Bigfoot" Wallace, a Texas Ranger who fought in the Mexican War and other military conflicts of the Republic of Texas and the United States. Because of Wallace's contributions to the state's military efforts, he was eligible to receive a land grant as a reward for his service. Wallace signed the required forms and even persuaded Sam Houston, president of the Republic of Texas, to sign the documents entitling him to a grant of land on Galveston Island. However, the State of Texas blocked the land grant, forcing Wallace and his lawyer to spend years in court in a futile attempt to get what was rightfully his.

Photographs of Bigfoot Wallace bear a strong resemblance to the face on the wall of Ewing Hall. The face has resisted all attempts to remove it for many years. The "ghost face" was first sighted on the fourth-floor panel. To counter all of the morbid attention the face was attracting, the administration sandblasted it off the wall. A short time later, the image reappeared, this time on the third-floor panel. A second attempt to remove it failed as well. The bizarre image can now be seen on the second-floor panel. Whomever the face belongs to, he seems determined to remind the citizens of Galveston of the injustice that was perpetrated against him so many years ago.

THE FACE IN THE COURTHOUSE WINDOW

Carrollton, Alabama

Carrollton was incorporated on eighty acres of land in northwest Alabama on January 15, 1831. It was named for one of the signers of the Declaration of Independence, Charles Carroll. The first settlers included the Davis, Lanier, Stone and Johnston families. Carrollton would be just another sleepy little southern town were it not for its courthouse and its tragic legend.

The face of accused arsonist Henry Wells magically appeared on the garret window of the Pickens County Courthouse after he was lynched in 1878. *Marilyn Brown.*

Union general John T. Croxton's troops burned the original courthouse on April 5, 1865. After the war, the citizens of Carrollton spent eleven years raising the funds for the construction of a new wooden courthouse. Shortly after the new courthouse was erected, it burned down on November 16, 1876. The people of Carrollton were irate because their new courthouse had come to represent the restoration of their pride and dignity. Understandably, the sheriff of Pickens County was under a great deal of pressure to apprehend the arsonist, so he decided that Henry Wells, a mean-spirited black man with a criminal history who was known to carry a switchblade, was a likely candidate. Wells received word that the sheriff was looking for him, so he left town in a hurry. Two years later, Wells received word that his grandmother was gravely ill. When he returned to Carrollton under the cover of darkness, he was apprehended by the sheriff. According to a Georgia newspaper, the *Daily Inquirer*, Wells was captured on February 12, 1878. In the absence of a jail, Wells was held prisoner in the garret of the Pickens County Courthouse to await trial.

Shortly after his capture, Wells was looking out of the garret window one night when he saw a small group of men standing below his window. Over the next hour, more and more men arrived, turning the small crowd into an angry mob. Wells became really concerned when he noticed that one of the men was holding a rope. The story goes that as lightning flashed across the sky, Wells exclaimed, "I am an innocent man. If you hang me, I will be with you always." The men ignored his warning, probably because they could not hear him from up in the garret. Suddenly, several of them rushed up the stairs, grabbed Wells and dragged him down the stairs. Without ceremony, they lynched him from the pecan tree standing next to the courthouse.

The next morning, two members of the lynch mob were walking in front of the courthouse when they noticed someone looking down at them from the garret window. They ran up the stairs and were surprised to find that no one was up in the garret but them. In her book *13 Alabama Ghosts and Jeffrey*, author Kathryn Tucker Windham writes,

> *Through all the years, in spite of hail and storm, which destroyed all of the windows in the courthouse, this one pane remained intact. It has been scrubbed with soap and rubbed with gasoline by those who doubt its permanence, but it has met every test, and the face remains unchanged. At close range, the pane looks clear and flawless, but viewed from the ground, the fear-distorted face of Henry Wells can be clearly seen!*

THE GHOSTLY FACE AT FLAGLER COLLEGE

St. Augustine, Florida

Henry Morrison Flagler was an American financier and entrepreneur who was born in Hopewell, New York, on January 2, 1830. While working as a grain merchant in Bellevue, Ohio, in 1850, he began selling grain through John D. Rockefeller. Following an ill-fated attempt to manufacture salt, Flagler became a partner of Rockefeller's in the formation of what evolved into the Standard Oil Company. Then in 1883, Flagler merged several railroad lines in Florida. Through the creation of the Florida East Coast Railway, Flagler opened up Florida's east coast to development. In the late 1890s, he began building a chain of luxury hotels along his railway line, including the Cordova, the Alcazar and the Ponce de Leon in St.

Augustine. According to folklorists, Flagler's legacy in Florida goes beyond his business ventures.

Henry Flagler died on May 30, 1913, in Palm Beach. His coffin was transported to St. Augustine, where it lay in state in the rotunda of the Ponce de Leon Hotel. The story goes that as Flagler's body was being removed from the hotel after his funeral, a strong blast of wind blew the doors shut, leading some observers to conclude that Flagler's spirit was reluctant to leave the hotel. That afternoon, the workers who were cleaning up the rotunda noticed a strange shape on one of the floor tiles. On close examination, the image seemed to bear an uncanny resemblance to the face of Henry Flagler. Shivers rose up their spines when they realized that the ceramic tile was from the same general area where Flagler's coffin had been stored.

When the Ponce de Leon Hotel was built in 1885, it was considered one of the finest hotels in the nation with its more than five hundred rooms, its hand-painted murals and solid oak pillars. Today, the former hotel is

Flagler College is housed in the former Ponce de Leon Hotel, built by railroad magnate Henry Morrison Flagler. *Leonardo J. De Francesci.*

home to Flagler College, a private four-year liberal arts college. Founded in 1968, Flagler College offers twenty-nine majors, thirty-four minors and, some say, a glimpse of Henry Flagler's face, still evident in one of the tiles in the rotunda.

ROBERT MUSGROVE'S TOMBSTONE

Amory, Alabama

Robert Musgrove was born in Fayette County, Alabama, in 1866, only one year after the end of the Civil War, during which his family—and the country—were divided. Growing up, he developed a lifelong fascination with trains. Even as a boy, he decided that he would do what it took to become an engineer. He started out on the railroad at a very young age as a water boy for the work crews laying tracks. For many years, he worked as a conductor, brakeman and fireman. Finally, he achieved his all-consuming dream: he became an engineer on the St. Louis and San Francisco Railroad.

When he was in his thirties, Musgrove began thinking seriously about all the pretty girls he had seen on the line. He enjoyed the attention he received from his female admirers, all of whom found him handsome and dashing, but he eventually gave his heart to a beautiful young woman in Amory. One bright, sunny day in the spring of 1904, Musgrove asked her to be his wife, and she accepted his proposal. He was so happy that he blew the train whistle all the way from Memphis to Amory. Sadly, his happiness came to an abrupt end in April 1904 when his train collided with another train between Memphis and Amory. Robert Musgrove was killed instantly. A caravan of wagons met the train carrying his body at the train station in Whitfield. His family transported the coffin to Musgrove Chapel in Fayette County. Among the mourners was Musgrove's fiancée, who rode in a wagon driven by W.L. Moss. After the funeral service, the congregation filed out to the cemetery. Once the coffin had been buried, everyone walked out of the cemetery with the exception of Musgrove's fiancée. Family members recalled seeing her kneeling on the grave with her head bowed and her hands folded in her lap. Before rising from the ground, she whispered, "Robert, I'll never leave you."

For years afterward, the woman conducted a lonely vigil at the grave of her lost love. She placed fresh flowers on his grave every week. She also swept it clean of leaves and twigs and pulled the weeds. She continued to care for Musgrove's grave until the day she died. No one paid much attention to his grave afterward until one Sunday morning in 1962. People were leaving Musgrove Chapel when someone noticed something off on Robert Musgrove's tombstone. There on the obelisk was the dark image of a woman kneeling, just as Musgrove's fiancée had done year after year. When scrubbing failed to remove the image, the church hired a stonemason from Birmingham to sandblast it. He removed the image, but it returned a few weeks later. The stonemason returned to the cemetery and, once again, sandblasted the image of the woman, but it came back not long thereafter. Older members of the congregation were not surprised by the persistence of the dark figure on the tombstone because they recalled what his fiancée said on the day of Musgrove's funeral: "I'll never leave you."

2
THE DEVIL'S BRIDES

MARY INGELMAN

Winnsboro, South Carolina

Sometime before 1854, a lawyer named Phillip Edward Pearson published the story of the witch trial of Mary Ingelman in Fairfield County. In 1792, the superstitious nature of the citizens of Fairfield County was aroused by a couple of incidents. In a nearby county, the Gifted Brethren were prosecuted and eventually disbanded by the authorities for practicing hypnosis. The founder of the group was eventually hanged in Charleston for the crime of heresy. During the summer of that same year, an unusually large number of cattle became sick and died. Several human beings took ill as well. Of course, today, food spoilage caused by the summer heat and diseases spread by mosquitos would probably be determined as the cause. However, in the late eighteenth century, the citizens of Fairfield County were eager to pin the crime on a flesh-and-blood individual.

The most likely culprit, from the point of view of Winnsboro's frightened citizenry, was a German widow named Mary Ingelman. Pearson described Ingelman as a "neat, tidy, and decent old lady who had a working knowledge of pharmaceuticals." From her little shack, she made and sold baked goods. Mary also created healing remedies with the herbs she collected in the woods. After people and animals started getting sick, some superstitious people blamed her for cursing the town in order to make a tidy profit selling her medicine. Once the word *witchcraft* was bantered around, some people began accusing her of a number of bizarre crimes. A woman named Rosy Henley swore that Ingelman had cursed her and her sister by causing them to levitate. Ingelman's own son from a previous marriage, Adam Free, accused her of making his cow jump into the air and break its neck. A man named Master Collins claimed that Ingelman had transformed him into a horse so that she could ride him to a witch meeting.

Soon, witch fever spread throughout Fairfield County. Eventually, Mary Ingelman and three other women were transported to Thomas Hill's farm five miles south of Winnsboro. Hill appointed himself as the judge and a local named John Crossland as sheriff and executioner. Following depositions by their accusers, the four women were found guilty of the crime of witchcraft. Crossland then attempted to torture confessions out of the women by flogging them and burning the soles of their feet. When none of the women confessed, all four were set free. As Ingelman was leaving Hill's farm, she was attacked by a man who threw her to the ground and laid a heavy pine log across her neck. The next morning, a man walking down the path removed the log and saved Ingelman's life.

One or two of the other accused witches fled Fairfield County for fear of more persecution. Ingelman, on the other hand, wanted justice served. She appealed to a different judge, Reverend William Youngue, to arrest Crossland. After viewing the scars on her back and the burns on her feet, the judge decided to indict Crossland. The "sheriff" was found guilty of battery and fined five pounds, which he never paid. For many years, Mary Ingelman's ghost could be seen sitting on the steps of the courthouse, awaiting the justice that was not completely served in her lifetime.

GRACE SHERWOOD

Pungo Beach, Virginia

A belief in witchcraft came across the Atlantic with the first colonists in Virginia. Nineteen years after the Jamestown colony was established in 1607, Goodwife Joan Wright was tried as a witch, based on the allegation that she had predicted the deaths of three women. She was also accused of taking revenge on a woman who had refused to hire her as a midwife by inflicting her with a strange sickness. The judge's verdict in the trial is unknown. In Virginia, the fear of witches was based more on superstition and folklore than on religious beliefs. The law required proof of guilt, either through search for witch marks or through "ducking," which involved immersing the accused in water to see if she would float. Of the nineteen cases involving witchcraft that were tried in Virginia in the seventeenth century, all but one ended with acquittal. Ducking was employed in only one of these cases—the trial of Grace Sherwood.

The charges of witchcraft against Grace Sherwood began in the late seventeenth century. In 1697, a farmer named Richard Capps accused her of casting a spell on his bull and killing it; she responded by suing Capps for defamation of character. The case ended in a settlement. A year later, Sherwood was accused of cursing John Gisburne by enchanting his cotton crop and his pigs. No legal action was taken against her in this case. A few months later, Elizabeth Barnes told officials that Sherwood had transformed herself into a cat, entered Barnes's bedroom, jumped on her and whipped her. Barnes claimed Sherwood then changed herself into a much smaller creature and escaped through the keyhole. Court action was not brought against Sherwood in this case either. Sherwood and her husband sued Gisburne and Barnes for defamation, but the couple lost both cases and were forced to pay court costs.

Sherwood's reputation as a witch continued to plague her in the dawn of the eighteenth century. In 1705, Sherwood got into a physical altercation with Elizabeth Hill. Grace and her husband sued Hill for assault and battery. The court decided in the Sherwoods' favor and awarded them damages of one pound sterling. Elizabeth Hill and her husband retaliated by accusing Sherwood of bewitching her and causing her to have a miscarriage. Sherwood was formally accused of witchcraft on February 7, 1706. She was to be tried by two juries composed of women. One jury was assigned the task of searching Sherwood's house for evidence of witchcraft, such as wax figures; the jury was instructed to examine Sherwood's body and look specifically for "the devil's teat." The juries were reluctant to carry out their duty, so on March 7, 1706, a special jury of twelve "ancient and knowing women" were told to look for marks of the devil on Sherwood's body. The jury concluded that her body bore marks unlike those found on any other woman. Not surprisingly, the foreman of the jury was Sherwood's old nemesis, Elizabeth Barnes.

On May 2, 1706, the justices at Pungo ruled that there was no hard proof of Sherwood's crime, but there was "great cause of suspicion." She was taken into custody by the sheriff of Princess County. On July 10, 1706, Sherwood was taken to a plantation near the mouth of the Lynnhaven River, where she was to undergo trial by water. She would be found guilty of witchcraft if she floated. While the crowd shouted "Duck the witch!," a sack was placed on Sherwood's head. She was then placed in a boat and rowed to a spot in the river two hundred yards from there. Her right thumb was tied to her right big toe, and her left thumb was tied to her right big toe. Then she was pushed into the river. Sherwood immediately floated to the surface, so the sheriff tied a thirteen-pound Bible around her neck and threw her back in the water again. Before sinking to the bottom, Sherwood managed to untie herself and rise to the surface once again. Sherwood was pulled out of the river. While rain poured downward on the onlookers, several women examined her for witch's teats.

The details of Sherwood's post-trial life are sketchy because many of the court records have not survived. She was "detained" in jail for a while to await a future trial, but no record of a follow-up trial exists. In 1714, Sherwood was ordered to pay back taxes on her property on Muddy Creek. The remainder of her life was uneventful.

Grace Sherwood passed away at age eighty in 1740. According to legend, her sons placed her body near the fireplace. Suddenly, a strong breeze whistled down the fireplace, causing the embers to flame up. All that remained when the fire died down was a cloven hoofprint. Other

This memorial to accused witch Grace Sherwood was erected on property owned by Old Donation Church in Virginia Beach, Virginia. *Pumpkin Sky*.

supernatural events are said to have occurred on the day of her death. Some people believe that the devil claimed her body and dragged her to hell. Others say that a tremendous thunderstorm arose and black cats congregated around her house. Grace Sherwood is buried in an unmarked grave near the intersection of Pungo Ferry Road and Princess Anne Road in Virginia Beach. Locals say that every July, a ghost light flits around the spot where she was thrown into the water in Witch Duck Bay.

Ironically, the demonic aura that hovered over Grace Sherwood's name has been dissipated by the passing of time. Local landmarks such as Witchduck Road and Witchduck Point commemorate Sherwood's trial. A play reenacting Sherwood's trial is performed at Colonial Williamsburg annually. A statue of Grace Sherwood has been erected near the site of the jail where she was incarcerated. In 2006, Grace Sherwood was given an official pardon by Governor Tim Kaine, three hundred years after her trial by water.

MARIE LAVEAU

New Orleans, Louisiana

Born on September 10, 1794, Marie Laveau was the illegitimate daughter of Charles Laveau, a rich politician, surveyor and plantation owner, and his mistress, Marguerite Henry, a woman of African, Choctaw and French descent. Marie was raised as a Catholic on her father's plantation and trained as a hairdresser. At age eighteen, Marie married Jacques Paris, a carpenter and free man of color from Haiti. At the time of her marriage, Laveau was a statuesque beauty with black, curly hair, golden skin and "white features." Her husband disappeared from Marie's life in 1824, leaving her with their two daughters, Felicite and Angela, to raise on her own. She supported her little family by working for the wealthy Creole and white women of New Orleans as a hairdresser. She also served as a nurse who may have performed minor operations.

In 1826, Marie moved in with Christophe Dominick Duminy de Glapion, a white man from a prominent New Orleans family. Marie and Glapion, whom she never married, had fifteen children together. Following Glapion's death in 1855, Marie ceased working as a hairdresser so that she could devote more time to her children.

Located in St. Louis Cemetery No. 1, the tomb of Marie Laveau is one of New Orleans's most popular grave sites. *James Gandolfo*.

At the time Marie had settled down into the life of a homemaker, she also embarked on a new career as a practitioner of voodoo. She was mentored by a local voodoo doctor known as "Doctor John" or "John Bayou." By 1830, Marie had established herself as the premier voodoo queen of New Orleans. She officiated over voodoo ceremonies performed at Congo Square. She also supervised the secret voodoo meetings held at the "Maison Blanche" (the White House). Marie's voodoo practices were a combination of Haitian voodoo and Catholicism. Laveau stressed the existence of spiritual forces that could be reached through dancing, singing and snake handling. From her cottage on St. Anne Street in the French Quarter, she performed exorcisms and voodoo rituals. On the side, she sold amulets called gris-gris, as well as charms and potions. She told fortunes and advised her clients on their love lives. In recent years, scholars have speculated that Marie's success as a diviner may have been due to the network of contacts she made in the homes of rich clients while working as a hairdresser. Although Marie instilled fear and awe in both her competitors and her admirers, she was also known for her humanitarian work. Laveau retired in 1875 and died on June 15, 1881, at the age of eighty-six.

Marie Laveau was buried in the Glapion family crypt in St. Louis Cemetery No. 1. According to local legend, visitors would have their wishes granted if they drew three Xs on the tomb, turned around three times, knocked on the tomb and stated their wish. If their wishes were granted, they would show their gratitude by drawing a circle around the Xs and leaving an offering. To prevent vandalism, local preservationists declared her tomb off-limits to everyone except tour groups on March 1, 2015.

THE BELL WITCH

Adams, Tennessee

In the early 1800s, John Bell moved from North Carolina to Tennessee. He and his wife, Lucy, settled on a farm in the town of Red River, now known as Adams. Over the next few years, he increased his holdings to 328 acres. By 1813, John and his wife had three children: Elizabeth "Betsy," Richard and Joel. The Bell family's peaceful existence was shattered forever one fateful day in 1817 when Bell was walking through his field with his gun. Out of the corner of his eye, he noticed a strange creature with the body of a dog and the head of a rabbit. Startled, he fired at the animal, which disappeared in a cloud of smoke. Later that evening, the Bell family began hearing scratching and rapping sounds on the outside of their log cabin. The supernatural activity escalated over the next few weeks. Elizabeth seemed to be the primary target of the vengeful spirit. She was pinched, slapped and stuck with pins by an invisible hand. Other family members were kicked and had their hair pulled. Blankets were yanked off beds, and pillows were thrown across the floor during the night. Bell tried to keep his "family troubles" secret at first, but eventually, he confided in a friend, who told several other neighbors. As soon as Bell's neighbors began assisting him with investigating the disturbances, the spirit began vocalizing. It identified itself as the "witch" of Kate Batts, a neighbor whom Bell had angered over the purchase of several slaves. Her spirit began making its presence known every day by quoting scripture, singing hymns and making conversation with Bell.

Rumors of the unearthly goings-on at the Bell farm soon spread throughout Tennessee and beyond. In 1819, General Andrew Jackson decided to experience the strange activity at the Bell farm personally. He and his entourage were pulling up to John Bell's house when, all of a sudden, the wheels of the wagon the men had brought along refused to turn. Jackson immediately exclaimed, "It must be the witch!" A voice that seemed to come out of nowhere responded by telling Jackson that he and his men could move on now. Instantly, the wagon's wheels began turning. Jackson arrived at Bell's front door a few minutes later. Bell welcomed Jackson inside, and the two men began to talk. Meanwhile, Jackson's men waited outside for signs of the witch. A self-proclaimed "witch tamer" whom Jackson had brought with him was showing his friends a silver bullet that he intended to use against the witch when he began jerking around violently. All at once, something kicked him from behind, causing him to sprawl on the ground. While the men stared at their friend in horror, a disembodied voice called the witch tamer a "fraud." Terrified, the men begged Jackson to leave. The entourage departed for Nashville early the next morning.

John Bell's health declined dramatically during the family's persecution by the Bell Witch. For an entire year, Bell's face began twitching uncontrollably. During the fall of 1820, he was afflicted with bouts of a strange sickness, during which the witch cursed and prodded him. On December 20, Bell was found lying in bed, senseless. A strange bottle was lying on the bed. A family member placed a drop of the foul-smelling liquid on the tongue of a cat;

This replica of John Bell's Cabin can be found at the Bell Witch Cave and Farm Location in Adams, Tennessee. *Brian Stansberry.*

it dropped dead immediately. Bell himself died not long thereafter. As Bell took his last breath, Kate Batts screamed triumphantly.

The Bell Witch continued tormenting the Bell family during the funeral, disrupting the service by laughing, cursing and singing. Her harassment of the family did not end with John Bell's burial. In April 1821, the Bell Witch told Lucy Bell that she would return in seven years. True to her word, the spirit manifested itself once again in 1827 and formed a relationship with John Bell Jr. The pair were said to have had long conversations on a wide variety of topics. The entity remained for three weeks before bidding John Bell Jr. farewell and vowing to return in 107 years. In a sense, the vengeful spirit did come back in the form of a book written by a descendant of John Bell, Dr. Charles Baily Bell, in 1934.

3

MYSTERIOUS DISAPPEARANCES

WHAT REALLY HAPPENED TO THEODOSIA BURR?

Nags Head, North Carolina

Aaron Burr will forever be known as the man who shot and killed former treasury secretary Alexander Hamilton. Lovers of unsolved mysteries, however, know him as the father of Theodosia Burr. Born in 1783, Theodosia grew up with her father and mother, Theodosia Prevost Burr. After her mother died, she became the hostess of the family estate at Richmond Hill, entertaining such notables as George Washington and Thomas Jefferson. In 1801, she married Joseph Alston, a handsome southern aristocrat, and went to live with him at his estate, the Oaks, in South Carolina. Not long after Theodosia's son, Aaron Burr Alston, was born in May 1802, her husband was elected governor of South Carolina.

Theodosia's happiness was relatively short-lived. Her responsibilities as first lady negatively affected her fragile health. During her father's conspiracy trial in 1807, she provided him with moral support, but the stress took a heavy toll on her. When her son died of tropical fever in 1812, she collapsed. A few months later, Aaron invited his daughter to visit him in New York in the hope that the trip would help ease the trauma of her son's death. John Alston was unable to leave South Carolina because of business matters, so Theodosia had to make the voyage alone. As the ship, the *Patriot*, sailed out

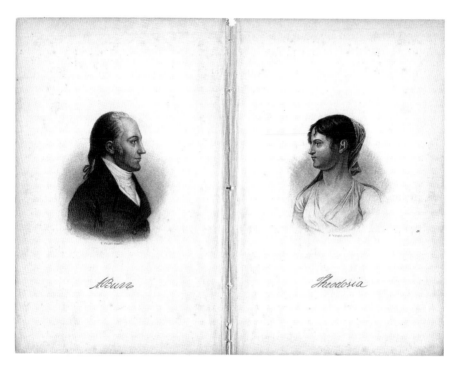

Theodosia Burr, daughter of Aaron Burr, was lost at sea at age twenty-nine. *Museum of American Finance.*

of Charleston Harbor on December 30, 1812, Alston was overcome with fear for his wife's safety. Not only were England and America at war, but pirates were rumored to be prowling around the Outer Banks as well.

John Alston's concern was well founded. Neither the *Patriot* nor any of the passengers were ever heard from again. Many people assumed that the ship was lost in a storm. Some, though, suspected that Theodosia Burr and the other passengers were victims of foul play. Their suspicions were confirmed—to an extent—in the 1830s. In 1833, a former pirate confessed to a reporter writing for an Alabama newspaper that he and his fellow pirates had plundered the *Patriot* and killed everyone onboard. Then in 1836, two pirates were arrested and taken to Norfolk, Virginia, for trial. Just prior to their hanging, the two men admitted that they and their shipmates had lured the *Patriot* on the rocks at Nags Head, North Carolina. Once the ship had foundered, the pirates forced all of the passengers to walk the plank. Their story was confirmed by Benjamin F. Burdick, who said that Theodosia Burr was the last passenger to walk the plank. Years later, the stricken look on the woman's face as she made her walk still haunted him. He remembered that she was clutching a Bible as she sank beneath the waves. Historians reject his story because she and her father were not religious people.

Another strange account of Theodosia's death centers on the grave of a "female stranger" in the graveyard at St. Paul's Episcopal Church in Alexandria, Virginia. Legend has it that a sickly woman and a man who claimed to be her husband arrived in Alexandria in 1816. When the physician arrived, the couple refused to give their names. The woman died of an undisclosed illness. To this day, some locals believe that they were actually John and Theodosia Alston.

The mystery deepened in 1869 when a doctor named William Poole and his daughter, Anna, visited the hone of one of his patients, Polly Mann, in Nags Head. As they entered the house, their eyes focused on the striking portrait of a beautiful young woman around twenty-five years old. Mrs. Mann told them that her late husband had found the painting in the cabin of an abandoned vessel that had drifted ashore. Dr. Poole took the painting in lieu of payment and showed it to members of the Burr family, but none of them was able to confirm that it was indeed the likeness of Aaron Burr's daughter.

THE CASE OF THE MISSING MILLIONAIRE

Vicksburg, Mississippi

The narrative of most of Jacqueline Levitz's life reads like a Cinderella story. She grew up as one of nine children on a cotton farm in Oak Grove, Louisiana. Life was hard for her and her siblings, each of whom routinely picked up to three hundred pounds of cotton in a single day. After high school, Jacqueline moved to Texas, where she attended secretarial school. She married Walter Bolton Jr. and had a son by him, Walter III. Following her divorce, she moved to Washington, D.C., and found employment in a real estate office. Her second marriage was to a successful restaurant owner, Banks L. Smith. After he died, Jacqueline moved to Florida. In 1987, she married Ralph Levitz, the wealthy owner of a furniture company. She embraced the life of a socialite, attending charity balls and throwing lavish parties at her $9 million oceanfront palace. The Levitzes' social life was curtailed in the last five years of Ralph's life by a series of strokes. Following her husband's death in March 1995, sixty-two-year-old

Jacqueline inherited a trust fund between $5 million and $15 million. The will dictated that Ralph's grandchildren from previous marriages would inherit the money after Jacqueline's death. She decided to make a new life for herself in Mississippi. She moved to a three-room ranch house situated on a bluff in Vicksburg. She then set about adding four bedrooms onto her modest home to accommodate visiting family members. During the remodeling, her furnishings consisted of plastic lawn chairs, a mattress and a refrigerator. Instead of socializing, Jacqueline spent most of her time supervising the forty-man construction crew, making sure that the work was going according to her specifications. During her entire time at Vicksburg, she attended only one social event—a Mary Kay party.

On November 18, 1995, Jacqueline went to town to purchase wallpaper. The store clerk was the last person to see her alive. Two days later, some of her relatives who had been trying unsuccessfully to contact her decided to check up on her at her home. As they walked to the house, they immediately sensed that something was wrong because the front door was open. When they entered the house, they could tell immediately that there had been a violent struggle. Broken false fingernails littered the floor; a bloodstained mattress had been overturned to hide a pool of blood on the floor. Interestingly enough, her furs, jewelry and expensive gowns were untouched.

Because of Jacqueline's immense wealth, the authorities immediately suspected foul play. The FBI was notified to investigate the possibility that she had been kidnapped. Agents also interviewed her family and friends in Florida, California and Washington, D.C. Her son was never considered to be a suspect because he was thousands of miles away when his mother disappeared. The police could find no evidence that anyone had ever threatened Jacqueline's life. The detectives considered the possibility that her body could have been buried on the shore. Her lawyer suspected that Jacqueline's disappearance was actually "a kidnapping that went terribly wrong." Jacqueline's personal psychic envisioned two men raping and murdering the heiress at the direction of one of her business associates. Jacqueline's sister, Tiki Shivers, suspected that someone followed her home from Wal-Mart and did away with her. To this day, her disappearance remains an unsolved mystery.

WHERE IS BOBBY DUNBAR?

St. Landry Parish, Louisiana

Bobby Dunbar was born in 1908 to Lessie and Percy Dunbar in Opelousas, Louisiana. On August 23, 1913, four-year-old Bobby accompanied his parents and his younger brother, Alonzo, on a trip to Swayze Lake in St. Landry Parish. While his parents were preoccupied, Bobby Dunbar wandered off unnoticed. By the time they discovered that their son was missing, it was too late. Bobby was nowhere to be found.

Local authorities combed the entire lake for any sign of the missing boy. Thinking that Bobby might have been the victim of an alligator attack, the police killed several of the reptiles and opened their stomachs. The police even dynamited the lake in the hope that the explosions would dislodge the boy's corpse. After a few days, the men found a set of bare footprints leading to a railroad trestle. Several local residents recalled seeing a strange man prowling around the lake on the day Bobby disappeared, leading the Dunbars to believe that their son might have been kidnapped. Touched by the Dunbars' plight, the town raised a $1,000 reward for Bobby's safe return.

The authorities decided to broaden the search for Bobby Dunbar after no trace of the boy was found around Swayze Lake. Percy Dunbar had descriptions of Bobby Dunbar printed on postcards, which were distributed to police departments from east Texas to Florida. After eight months, the authorities received word from Hub, Mississippi, that a man named William Cantwell Walters had been seen walking through town with a little boy. Walters told police that the boy's name was Charles Bruce Anderson and that his mother, Julia Anderson, had granted him custody of the boy. Julia was working for Walters's family at the time. The police found Walters's story to be far-fetched and arrested him. Meanwhile, the Dunbars traveled to Hub, Mississippi, to retrieve their son. Lessie was not sure that the boy really was Bobby until she bathed him and recognized several identifying moles and scars. With the blessing of the local authorities, the Dunbars loaded the child into their car and returned to Louisiana.

However, the boy's "return" to the Dunbars' home turned out to be only the beginning of the mystery. Julia Anderson traveled to Opelousas to lay claim to her son. She informed the police that she had given Walters permission to take her son for only a two-day trip to one of his relatives. The police decided to test the validity of her story by placing the boy in a lineup of boys the same age and asking Julia to identify her son. Because Julia was unable to do so, the boy was returned to the Dunbars.

Julia Anderson returned to Louisiana for Walters's trial. He was found guilty of kidnapping after a two-week trial and was sentenced to life in prison. Walters spent only two years in jail, however, because the town was reluctant to spend any more money on the case.

The boy whom Julia Anderson had insisted was her son was raised as Bobby Dunbar. He eventually married and had four children before dying in 1966. In 2004, the Dunbar children decided that it was time to prove once and for all that their father really was Bobby Dunbar. Robert Dunbar Jr., Bobby's son, agreed to have his DNA sample compared with that of a cousin, Alonzo Dunbar's son. The samples did not match. The fate of the real Bobby Dunbar remains unknown.

VANISHED IN THE SMOKY MOUNTAINS

Chattanooga, Tennessee

On June 5, 1969, Dennis Martin and his family were vacationing in Cade's Cove, just as they had for years. On this particular day, they were visiting a scenic spot known as Spence Field. Dennis, who was just a few days away from his seventh birthday, was playing near the top of Anthony Creek trailhead with his brother Douglass and two other boys. When nine-year-old Douglass spotted his father and several other adults sitting around talking, he and the other boys decided to play a joke on them. Their plan was for Douglass and the other two boys to sneak around one side of the group, while Dennis sneaked around the other side. Then all four boys would jump up and surprise the grownups. When the boys reappeared, Dennis was nowhere to be seen,

After a few minutes, William Martin began calling his son's name, but there was no reply. He walked up the trail to Little Bald and then took another trail in the opposite direction to Russell Field. At 8:30 p.m., park rangers were notified of the missing child. At the time of the boy's disappearance, Dennis was wearing green short pants, a red T-shirt and Oxford shoes. As darkness began to blanket the mountain and the rain began to fall, the search was called off.

The next day was the beginning of what was to become the largest search effort in the history of Great Smoky Mountains National Park. Approximately 1,400 volunteers from Georgia, Kentucky and North and South Carolina climbed up and down Lookout Mountain, searching for any sign of the boy. Even the military participated in the search, including members of the U.S. Special Forces from Fort Bragg and two Huey helicopters. Medics, the Boy Scouts and college students joined in the search. For a short while, William Martin flew over Cade's Cove in a single-engine U-10 airplane with a loudspeaker until the rear landing gear hit a rock, damaging the plane. A Tennessee Highway Patrol helicopter resumed the search from the air with a bullhorn the next day. Even psychic Jeanne Dixon offered to search for the boy through her visions. No leads were ignored.

After covering fifty-seven square miles, the search was terminated on September 14, 1969. Approximately 13,430 search hours and $50,584 were spent on the hunt for the boy. Ironically, the manpower involved in such a massive search effort could have inadvertently trampled on Dennis Martin's footprints.

Over the years, no trace of Dennis Martin has been found, despite the fact that his father offered a $5,000 reward for information. Several years after the official search for Dennis Martin was called off, a local ginseng hunter discovered the skeleton of a child in Big Hollow. He told no one of his find until 1985 for fear of prosecution. Forensics determined that the bones were not those of Dennis Martin.

Several theories have been proposed for Dennis Martin's disappearance. Some people believe Dennis wandered off the main trail, got lost and died of exposure on the first night. The possibility also exists that he was killed by a bear or a feral pig. Dennis's father believes his son was kidnapped. A tourist named Harold Key told investigators that around the time when the boy disappeared, he heard what he described as "an enormous, sickening scream." He then observed a "rough-looking man" walking through the woods before climbing into a white car and driving off. The police dismissed Key's statement as being irrelevant because he was five miles away from the place where Dennis Martin disappeared when he noticed the stranger. The fate of the little boy is still unknown.

ROANOKE, THE LOST COLONY

Dare County, North Carolina

In 1584, Sir Walter Raleigh sent Captain Philip Amadas and Arthur Barlowe on a voyage to explore the North American coast. At the time, England was eager to establish a foothold in North America by setting up permanent colonies. As a result of Amadas and Barlowe's favorable report, Raleigh sent 108 colonists to Roanoke Island in what is now Dare County, North Carolina, in 1585. A year later, the lack of supplies and the constant threat of attack by the native inhabitants prompted most of the colonists to return to England, leaving behind only a small group of men. By the time John White led a second expedition to Roanoke in July 1587, the small detachment of colonists had vanished. While White was there, his granddaughter, Virginia Dare, was born, becoming the first English child born in the New World. He returned to England later in the year to secure government assistance for the colony. Because of the Anglo-Spanish War, however, White could not return to Roanoke for three years. When White was finally able to sail back to Roanoke, he was shocked to find that the entire colony had disappeared. During their search, White's men found the letters "CRO" carved on a tree. On further investigation, they learned that all of the colonists' houses had been pulled down and that the area had been enclosed by a palisade of trees. On one of these "tree posts" was carved the word "Croatoan." White's party was disturbed by the absence of the Maltese cross on the post, which the colonists were supposed to include with all messages if they were in danger.

Nevertheless, the evidence reassured White that his granddaughter and the other colonists would be found on Croatoan Island. However, White and his party were prevented from visiting Croatoan Island by a powerful storm. Reluctantly, White's party had to call off its search and return to England.

White was unable to finance another expedition to America, but Sir Walter Raleigh continued to send ships to search for the Lost Colony. Many historians believed that these expeditions concentrated on trading with the local natives instead of looking for the Roanoke colonists. After Jamestown Plantation was founded in 1607, the colonists asked the native tribes for information about the Lost Colony but were unable to learn anything substantive about the colonists' fate.

A number of explanations have been proposed for the disappearance of the Roanoke colonists. Early on, the most popular theory was that the

This painting depicts the baptism of Virginia Dare, the first English child born in the New World. Her fate and the fate of the other Roanoke colonists are unknown. *William A. Crafts.*

colony was massacred by Indians, even though no corpses were ever found. Another theory holds that the colonists made an ill-fated attempt to sail back to England on their own and drowned. The possibility that Spaniards who had marched up to North Carolina from Florida murdered the English has also been considered. In recent years, some researchers have proposed that the colonists were abducted by the Indians and absorbed into the tribe. The Lumbees are the most likely possibility because one of their oral traditions traces the tribe's ancestry back to the Lost Colony. This hypothesis is bolstered by the prevalence of several English names in the tribe today, such as Allen, Berry, Graham, Martin and White.

4

MYSTERIOUS INJURIES
AND DEATHS

THE CASE OF THE "HOT" MATH PROFESSOR

Nashville, Tennessee

On January 5, 1835, a highly esteemed math professor at the University of Nashville named James Hamilton walked home after work, just as he had done countless times before. After adding wood to the fire in the fireplace, he went to the other side of his room and checked his thermometer and barometer. A half hour later, Hamilton stepped outside to check the wind direction on his hygrometer. He was standing around for approximately ten minutes when he felt a deep pain on his thigh. At first, he thought he had been stung by a hornet. Hamilton glanced down at his leg and was shocked to find a circle of flame on his pants. He tried to extinguish the flame by slapping it, but to no avail. Finally, the professor decided to cup his hands over the tiny flame and deprive it of oxygen. Within a matter of seconds, the flame had died down.

Thinking that his pants had caused the burning, Hamilton pinched the material away from the locus of his pain. Within a few minutes, the pain diminished, but at the same time, the area around the spot felt very warm. Hamilton removed his pants and underwear and took a close look at the place where he had felt the most pain. His wound appeared to be an abrasion three inches long and three-fourths of an inch wide. Hamilton then examined his clothes. His pants were not burned at all. In his underwear, however, was a hole. Strangely, the area around the hole did not appear to have been singed.

Convinced that the wound was not serious, Hamilton decided not to treat it. The next morning, though, the pain returned, so he rubbed salve on the spot. Over the next five days, the pain intensified, so Hamilton made an appointment with a local physician, Dr. Overton. The doctor said that the healing process would be slow because the injury was so deep. Hamilton was not fully healed until thirty-two days later. The pain was gone, but an ugly scar was left behind. Dr. Overton was surprised that this type of wound had produced such a deep scar. Baffled as to the true cause of the injury, Dr. Overton referred to it as "partial spontaneous combustion" in his report.

MARY REESER'S STRANGE DEATH

St. Petersburg, Florida

At 9:00 p.m. on July 1, 1951, a sixty-seven-year-old widow named Mary Reeser said good night to her landlady, Pansy M. Carpenter, and her son, Dr. Richard Reeser. When her company left her apartment, Mrs. Reeser was sitting in her easy chair. Nothing appeared to be out of the ordinary. The next morning, Mrs. Carpenter woke up to the pungent odor of smoke at 5:00 a.m. She concluded that the water heater had overheated, so she turned it off and returned to bed. Three hours later, the telegraph boy knocked on the door, waking her up. He handed her a telegraph for Mrs. Reeser. After signing for it, Mrs. Carpenter walked over to Mrs. Reeser's house and knocked on the door. No one answered. She touched the doorknob but removed her hand immediately because of the intense heat. Mrs. Carpenter ran down the street and asked a couple of house painters to accompany her back to Mrs. Reeser's house.

With a great deal of effort, the men forced the door open. They were met by a blast of air that sent them reeling back on their heels. When they regained their composure, they looked into the room. What they saw filled them with horror. All that was left of Mrs. Reeser's 170-pound body was a 10-pound charred mass, with the exception of her left foot. On closer inspection, investigators discovered later on that her liver was fused to her vertebrae and her skull was reduced to the size of a teacup. Only the small corner where she had placed her easy chair was touched by the flames. Soot covered the walls throughout the apartment; a plastic tumbler and all of the light switches were melted. All that remained of two candles was a pink pool of melted wax. Her clock had stopped at 4:20 a.m. The investigators ruled out smoking as the cause of the fire because a temperature of 2,500 degrees is required for cremation of a human body. They decided that faulty wiring was not the cause because the electrical outlet melted after the fire had started. However, for lack of a better explanation, the chief of police attributed the cause of the fire to Mrs. Reeser's having fallen asleep holding a cigarette.

In recent years, several cases of spontaneous combustion have been determined to be the result of the "Wick Effect." According to scientists, a small fire on the body can ignite a victim's body fat in a slow, intense flame. Mrs. Reeser was a smoker. Her left foot was not consumed in the flames because she had extended it away from her body. Skeptics, on the other hand, point out that heads do not shrink when heated—they explode. Some people believe that Mrs. Reeser's "skull" was actually a knot of muscle from the back of her neck. The coroner, they say, misidentified it as bone because the charring had hardened the muscle. The shrunken skull is the only aspect of this case that could be paranormal in origin.

THE CONTROVERSIAL DEATH OF DAVY CROCKETT

San Antonio, Texas

The Battle of the Alamo in San Antonio is one of the most stirring events in American history. Between February 23 and March 6, 1836, the 200 defenders made a valiant stand against General Santa Anna's 2,064 troops. On March 6, Santa Anna finally succeeded in breeching the walls of the Alamo. The defenders fell back to the church, the convent and the adobe apartments while their attackers fired on them with their own cannons. The Mexican soldiers then proceeded to search each room, bayonetting and shooting everything that moved; 60 defenders escaped but were shot down on Gonzales Road. Davy Crockett, with a terrible gash, stood in front of a pile of Mexican soldiers he had killed and faced his assailants with a rifle in his right hand and a bloody bowie knife in his left. Suddenly, Crockett was completely overwhelmed by a gang of soldiers, taking down as many

For years, scholars have questioned the traditional, heroic portrayal of Davy Crockett's death on March 6, 1836, at the Alamo. *Nuggehalli2015.*

as he could with the rifle he was swinging. This is the standard version of the story of Crockett's death that has been passed down to generations of schoolchildren. However, evidence has surfaced suggesting that Crockett's actual death might have been far less heroic.

Challenges to the romanticized account began surfacing only a few years after the battle. In 1859, Dr. Nicholas Labadie claimed that he was told by Colonel Fernando Urriz that a man called "Coket" was shot by a file of soldiers. Sergeant Francisco Becerra told reporters in 1875 that Crockett and Travis were shot by a firing line. In 1890, the wife of Candelario Villanueva reported that Crockett was one of the first to be shot while running from the church toward the wall. She added that he was carrying no weapons when he died. In 1896, a woman named Eulailia Yorba said that she was tending to a dying man when she recognized Crockett lying next to him. Crockett had been killed with the thrust of a bayonet or a ball in chest. That same year, historian William P. Zuber reported receiving information regarding Mexican general Martin Perfecto de Cos, who brought Crockett to Santa Anna and pleaded his case. When the general refused to offer leniency and ordered his execution, Crockett lunged at him with a large knife. A guard standing nearby bayonetted Crockett in the heart.

In 1955, the same year that Disney released the movie *Davy Crockett, King of the Wild Frontier*, the diary of Lieutenant José Enrique de la Peña was published in Mexico. De la Peña claimed that he had participated in the siege of the Alamo and that Crockett was executed with swords. Because of the immense popularity of Disney's romanticized version of Crockett's death, a theory that did not portray the frontier hero swinging his rifle like a club in his last moments was not welcomed by the general public. By the time the diary was published by a university press in the United States, a number of prominent historians had found corroborating evidence from the Texan side of the conflict. In a letter written on March 11, 1836, General Sam Houston records, "After the fort was carried, seven men surrendered and called for Santa Anna and [mercy]. They were murdered by his order." Houston did not name Crockett as one of the prisoners. A member of Sam Houston's staff named Colonel James H. Perry reported in 1842 that, according to Bowie's slave, Crockett and six other companions were the last of the defenders of the Alamo still standing. They were ordered to surrender, but Crockett shouted defiantly and leaped into a crowd of soldiers, who stabbed him with a lance. Three weeks after the battle, passengers aboard the schooner *Comanche* told a newspaper reporter that Crockett and several other men had tried to surrender but were told by a Mexican officer that they would receive no mercy.

The death of Davy Crockett is still a contentious subject, especially in Texas and Tennessee, where the frontiersman has been raised to the status of a folk hero. Texas author Dan Kilgore took an unpopular stand on the issue in his book *How Did Davy Die?* Kilgore put great stock in the accounts of four Mexican officers and a sergeant who participated in the assault and observed the final tragedy: "[They] specifically identified Crockett as one of the captives….Their accounts have come to light over a long period of time, several having surfaced only recently. Any one of them, standing alone, could be subject to question, but considered as a whole, the statements provide stronger documentation than can be claimed for any other incident during the battle." In spite of the evidence produced by scholars, changing the minds of millions of Americans regarding the heroic death of one of the nation's most iconic figures will be difficult indeed. In 2004, Hollywood released another movie about the siege, *The Alamo*. In the end of the film, Davy Crockett and four other defenders make their last stand in the church. Crockett is captured and executed. Not surprisingly, the film was a box office flop.

THE MYSTERIOUS DEATH OF MERIWETHER LEWIS

Hohenwald, Tennessee

Meriwether Lewis will always be remembered as the leader of the Lewis and Clark Expedition, officially known as the Corps of Discovery. In 1803, President Thomas Jefferson assigned Lewis and William Clark the task of exploring the territory just acquired in the Louisiana Purchase, establishing relations with the Indians and laying claim to the Oregon Country and the Pacific Northwest for the United States. In 1806, Jefferson appointed Lewis governor of Upper Louisiana. Before long, it became clear that Lewis was much more effective as a soldier and explorer than as a politician. In September 1809, Lewis set out from his St. Louis headquarters for Washington, D.C., to take his papers and documents from his western explorations to be edited and published in Philadelphia or Washington. Even more pressing was his need to answer questions regarding the legitimacy of expenses he had incurred during the expedition in 1803. Lewis realized that if the bureaucrats and Washington forced him to cover these costs personally, he could be facing bankruptcy. Lewis's personal problems were exacerbated by alcoholism and several undiagnosed illnesses, which might have included malaria or syphilis.

Lewis and a small party had planned to travel by boat from New Orleans to Washington, but when he reached Chickasaw Bluffs, now known as Memphis, he decided to travel along the Natchez Trace instead because he heard that British ships were patrolling the Gulf of Mexico. On October 10, 1809, the party's packhorses ran off during a torrential thunderstorm, taking Lewis's precious records with them. His traveling companion, an Indian agent named Captain James Neely, urged Lewis to seek shelter while he and the servants tracked down the horses in the forest. Lewis decided to spend the night at a log cabin inn called Grinder's Stand. Instead of sleeping on the bed, which he feared was crawling with vermin, Lewis opted to make a pallet from a buffalo robe and sleep on the floor. The mistress of the tavern, Mrs. Grinder, told authorities later on that during the night, she heard Lewis pacing back and forth, followed by the words, "Oh, Lord!" A minute or so later, Mrs. Grinder heard a gunshot. Within a few moments, Lewis appeared outside her door, calling out to her, "Oh, Madame, give me some water and heal my wounds!" Staring through the chinks in the log walls, Mrs. Grinder saw Lewis stagger around and collapse between his bedroom and the kitchen. He crawled around at

The Meriwether Lewis Memorial is located at Meriwether Lewis Park Road in Hohenwald, Tennessee, on the Natchez Trace. The broken column symbolizes a life cut short. *Sky Marthaler*.

first; then he got up and walked unsteadily back to the kitchen, where he scraped a gourd dipper against the bottom of an empty bucket. Fearing for her life, Mrs. Grinder refused to assist Lewis. Instead, she ordered her children to go to the barn and wake up his servants.

The men rushed inside the inn and found Lewis lying on the blood-soaked pallet. They examined his body and found that he had a bullet hole in his abdomen. Even worse, part of his forehead had been blasted away. Lewis whispered to them, "I am no coward, but I am strong, so hard to die." By the time Mr. Grinder and Captain Neely arrived at mid-morning, Lewis was dead. Captain Neely immediately sent off a letter to President Jefferson, informing him of Lewis's apparent suicide. Lewis was buried on the Grinders' property. Neely saw to it that Lewis's recovered papers were returned to Washington and turned over to the state department.

Not everyone accepted Captain Neely's hasty explanation of Lewis's death. Suspicion was immediately placed on Grinder, who was suspected of killing and robbing the explorer. However, Lewis had only twenty-five cents on his person at the time, so robbery was ruled out as a motive. Grinder was arrested and charged with murder but was released due to the lack of evidence. Another of Lewis's traveling companions, a Creole named John Pernia, was also a person of interest, primarily because he vanished soon after Lewis's death. Another theory postulates that Captain Neely and several of Lewis's political enemies in St. Louis had conspired to have him killed, but once again, evidence could not be found.

For years, Meriwether Lewis lay in an unmarked graved in a wooded area just off the Natchez Trace. Today, his grave is marked by a broken column, signifying a life that was cut short far too soon at the age of thirty-five. Some visitors to the grave site claim to have seen Lewis's restless spirit wandering around his grave and muttering to himself, "It is so hard to die."

5

LEGENDARY GRAVES

THE MYSTERY GIRL'S LAST DANCE

Harrodsburg, Kentucky

In the 1840s, Harrodsburg, Kentucky, was like many other southern towns that prospered in the nineteenth century because of its underground springs. Each year, thousands of people vacationed here in the summertime to drink the curative waters of its mineral springs. Many of these visitors stayed at the Harrodsburg Springs Hotel at Graham Springs. The owners, Dr. and Mrs. C.C. Graham, went to great lengths to make their guests' stay at their establishment as pleasurable—and memorable—as possible. Guests walked down winding paths lined with flowers to the springhouses, where they chatted and drank the spring water. The grandest event at the Harrodsburg Springs Hotel was its nightly ball. Dancers glided around the floor of the immense ballroom, hoping to establish a social reputation and, possibly, find a suitable prospect for marriage. One of these balls provided the backdrop for a mystery that remains unsolved to this day.

The story goes that in the mid-nineteenth century, a beautiful young woman checked into the Harrodsburg Springs Hotel with a small trunk. She registered as Mary Virginia Stafford of Louisville, Kentucky. Knowing full well that ladies did not travel unescorted in the Deep South, she explained to the desk clerk that her parents, Judge and Mrs. Stafford, would arrive later that evening with the rest of her luggage. Even before she started climbing the stairs to her bedroom, several young men standing around the lobby asked her to dance with them later that evening. Miss Stafford only laughed and proceeded to her room. After supper, she walked into the ballroom wearing a striking evening gown. Immediately, she was surrounded by young men who, once again, bombarded her with requests for the next dance. For the remainder of the evening, Stafford danced with all of the eligible bachelors in the ballroom. Taking time to catch her breath during the intermission, she told one of her suitors, "I am having such a wonderful time. I wish I could stay here forever." When the band struck up again, she resumed dancing with everyone who asked her. Late in the evening, when the hotel manager announced, "This is the last dance," she walked out onto the ballroom floor with her final dance partner. Before the music ended, she collapsed in his arms, dead.

Before long, the hotel manager discovered that the name she had given was a fake. The contents of her trunk provided no evidence of her real name. Newspapers carrying the story of the girl who "danced herself to death" asked readers to supply any information they had regarding her true identity. Her funeral was arranged by hotel management. Her dance partners served as her pallbearers. Her grave at the edge of the city park is enclosed by a small white picket fence. The metal marker above the concrete slab reads, "Unknown—Hallowed and Hushed Be the Place of the Dead. Step softly…Bow Head."

The Harrodsburg Springs Hotel burned down years ago. Over the years, people claimed to have seen a young girl wearing an antebellum ball gown walking around the hotel site. In her book *Jeffrey Introduces 13 More Southern Ghosts*, Kathryn Tucker Windham writes that in the 1960s, a nurse taking a late-night walk near the springhouse reported that a girl in a white dress walked up to her. She seemed to be confused and disoriented. The figure walked up to the nurse and said, "Please help me! I was attending a ball at the hotel, but now, I can't find my way back." When the nurse explained that the hotel had burned down, the apparition buried her face in her hands and ran into the springhouse, where she vanished.

The girl's identity remained a complete mystery until 2003, when rumors surfaced that she might have been Mollie Black, the estranged wife of a man named Joe Sewell. The couple had a small son at the time of her death. He was brought up in the place of her birth—Laurel County, Kentucky—as "Miller." Although a Joe Sewell did live during this period, no trace of a Mollie Black has been found. In the absence of definitive documentation, "the girl who danced herself to death" remains one of the oldest Jane Does in American history.

THE HAUNTED MAUSOLEUM

Edisto Island, South Carolina

The first inhabitants of Edisto Island, one of South Carolina's sea islands, were the Edistow Indians. In the late nineteenth century, planters began buying up large tracts of land on the island. Most of these individuals made their living planting indigo and rice and raising free-ranging cattle. By 1860, Edisto Island's population consisted of 329 whites and 5,082 slaves. In 1861, most of the planters abandoned their plantations. By the end of the Civil War, only a handful of slaves and planters remained. Today, Edisto Island is primarily a tourist destination, although a few plantations—and plantation stories—remain.

Edisto Island's signature legend is the saga of Julia Legare. Her father, Captain William Seabrook, was one of the first planters to cultivate sea island cotton on the island. Aside from running several plantations, Seabrook also operated a ferryboat business. His daughter, Julia Georgianna Seabrook, was born to his second wife, Elizabeth Emma Eddings, on November 18, 1830, at the William Seabrook Plantation. Julia was said to be a sickly child who was in the constant care of the local physicians. Despite her frail health, Julia married John Berwick Legare in 1848. Four years later, Julia contracted malaria. When the doctors arrived, they found that she had slipped into a coma. Unable to find a pulse, they declared her dead on April 15, 1852. Julia was twenty-two years old. Her corpse was laid to rest in the family mausoleum behind the Presbyterian church. After closing the marble door, her loved ones assumed that this tragic chapter in their lives had come to an end.

The next part of the story exists in several variants. In one version, a caretaker passed by the Legare mausoleum a few days after the death and discovered that the door was standing wide open. In another version, mourners found that the door was open fifteen years later when they were preparing to bury a relative in the mausoleum; in another account, only two years had passed. The one story element that remains constant is what was discovered inside the mausoleum after it was opened. Lying in a corner were the skeletal remains of Julia Legare. Some people say that Julia's fingernails were broken. Scratch marks on the door led her family to the grisly conclusion that they had buried their daughter alive.

The mystery of the open door deepened in the months and years following the initial discovery of Julia Legare's remains. A few weeks later, a minister told the family that he found the mausoleum open once again while he was walking into the church. Over the years, attempts were made to keep the door shut using locks and chains, but the next day, the door was always found standing wide open. In the 1960s, a special door that could only be removed with specialized equipment was installed, but not long thereafter, it was lying on the ground, completely unhinged from the mausoleum.

These days, the door to the Legare family mausoleum is completely gone. Some passersby claimed that they saw the original door lying in a patch of weeds outside of the entrance. Others believe that the original marble door was found in pieces inside the mausoleum and remained on the floor of the mausoleum. Apparently, the open entrance to the mausoleum has not put Julia Legare's spirit to rest. Rumor has it that her ghost guards against any well-meaning attempts to replace the marble door. A few superstitious visitors have heard mournful cries coming from the direction of the mausoleum. Her legend will undoubtedly continue to be told as long as her mausoleum still stands.

JOHN ROWAN'S RESTLESS TOMBSTONE

Bardstown, Kentucky

John Rowan was one of the South's most prominent statesmen in the first half of the nineteenth century. He was so sickly as a child that his survival into adulthood was in doubt. Rowan's health greatly improved after his father moved his family to Kentucky. Rowan attended law school and was admitted to the bar in 1875. Afterward, he entered the world of politics, becoming a state judge, a U.S. senator, Kentucky's secretary of state and chief justice for the court of appeals. Aside from being a high-profile politician, Rowan was also known as the cousin of Stephen Foster, the composer of such popular songs as "I Dream of Jeannie with the Light Brown Hair," "Oh, Susanna" and "My Old Kentucky Home."

Rowan's privileged upbringing and elevated social status as an adult did not insulate him from personal tragedy. Rowan's insensitive comments about the wife of a friend of his, Dr. James Chambers, resulted in a duel, during which the doctor was killed. Then in 1833, a cholera epidemic took the lives of twenty-six slaves and four members of Rowan's family, including his son John, who had stopped by the mansion for a visit while traveling to Washington.

John Rowan passed away in July 1843. Before dying, he told his family that because his parents had been buried without a tombstone, he did not want one either. From his point of view, his beautiful home on Federal Hill was monument enough. However, Rowan's family ignored their father's final wishes, believing that a man of his standing deserved an appropriate grave marker.

Only a few days after Rowan was interred in Federal Hill Cemetery, the obelisk erected in his honor fell over. The stonemasons who set the obelisk back in place theorized that it had toppled over as the result of shifting sediment or tree roots. When the obelisk fell over again less than two months later, word spread through Bardstown that Rowan's family had angered their father's spirit by marking his grave. Not surprisingly, the obelisk fell over again not long after the stonemasons had made their repairs.

The monument fell so many times that the local stonemasons refused to prop it back up again. They were replaced by the cemetery workers, who knew that all of their efforts to violate the wishes of the grave's occupant would probably be in vain.

CRAIGMILES MAUSOLEUM

Cleveland, Tennessee

John Henderson Craigmiles was famous in the mid-nineteenth century for his business savvy. In 1850, he moved from Georgia to Cleveland, Tennessee, where he operated a mercantile with his brother, Pleasant. Tiring of life in a small town, he moved to California and tried to strike it rich mining for gold. Because prospecting was not what he had imagine it would be, he soon realized that he could make much more money in the shipping business. Craigmiles founded a shipping line between California and Panama. Later, he began carrying passengers as well. Craigmiles's shipping line was interrupted by the hijacking of five of his six ships. He lost his entire fortune but was able to restart his business with his one remaining ship. When he returned to Tennessee in 1857, he was, once again, a wealthy man.

Craigmiles had not lived in Cleveland very long before he fell in love with and married Adelia Thompson on December 18, 1860. During the Civil

War, he held the position of chief commissary agent for the South. Using his political connections, Craigmiles amassed another fortune by buying cattle and speculating in cotton. Concerned that Confederate currency would soon be worthless, he traded only in gold. Consequently, he was not ruined, as many Southern businessmen were at the end of the Civil War.

In August 1864, the Craigmileses' first daughter, Nina, was born. From the day her parents brought her home, Nina became the center of her family's attention. John and Adelia lavished love and attention on their daughter, but her maternal grandfather, Dr. Thompson, spoiled her more than anyone else. Every day, Nina accompanied him on his walks downtown and sat by his side when the doctor made house calls in his buggy. Nina's idyllic existence in Cleveland came to an abrupt—and tragic—end in October 1871. The little girl and her grandfather were taking a buggy ride downtown when they reached the railroad tracks. As they were crossing the tracks, the buggy suddenly veered into the path of an oncoming locomotive. Dr. Thompson was thrown clear, but Nina was killed instantly.

The death of the beloved seven-year-old girl devastated her family and the community as a whole. Following the funeral, John began formulating plans to erect a church as a memorial to his daughter. Because no Episcopal church had been built in Cleveland before Nina's death, the building project would satisfy an important spiritual need. Construction of St. Luke's Episcopal Church began in August and was finished on October 8, 1874. Work on the Craigmiles family mausoleum commenced soon afterward. The four-foot-thick walls of the mausoleum were made of the finest marble. A thirty-seven-foot spire was placed on top of the tomb. Nina's corpse occupied the center of the room; it was surrounded by six shelves built into the wall.

The extra spaces within the Craigmiles mausoleum began filling up within a few decades. Nina's father died of blood poisoning in January 1899 after slipping and falling on an icy street. Adelia, who had remarried, was hit and killed by a car while crossing a street in September 1928.

The Craigmileses' bloody family history is said to be embedded in the very walls of the mausoleum. Soon after Nina's death, faint red streaks appeared on the mausoleum. The stains became visibly darker following the death of each consecutive family member. Many people believed that the stains had a supernatural origin. Over the years, the blood-colored stains resisted all attempts to remove them. Locals are fully aware that the sad history of the Craigmiles family will continue to be passed down as long as the red stains are still visible.

THE GRAVE OF STONEWALL JACKSON'S ARM

Chancellorsville, Virginia

Following the Union defeat at the Battle of Fredericksburg, Major General Joseph "Fighting Joe" Hooker moved his army above Fredericksburg in order to attack Robert E. Lee's army from the rear. Lee moved his army west toward a small country town called Chancellorsville. He immediately began maneuvering his men behind the wiry underbrush. On April 30, Hooker marched his men to the rear of the Confederate army. General Lee and General Thomas "Stonewall" Jackson decided to divide their forces by placing a rear guard at Fredericksburg. On May 2, Jackson moved his army around Hooker's army while Lee remained behind to face Hooker's forces. Late in the afternoon, Jackson's ragged soldiers charged out of the wilderness, yelling at the top of their lungs. Before long, Jackson had destroyed half of Hooker's line. By battle's end, the Confederacy had lost 12,800 men, and the Union army had suffered 17,000 casualties. The Battle of Chancellorsville turned out to be Lee's greatest victory, but it came at a heavy cost.

As night fell on May 2, Jackson and several of his staff officers were conducting reconnaissance around the battlefield. As the group neared the woods, they were fired on by a North Carolina regiment who mistook them for Yankees. Jackson was struck by three bullets, two of which shattered his left arm. Jackson was evacuated to a nearby field hospital and given medical attention. His left arm was amputated, but Jackson eventually contracted pneumonia and died. His body was transported to Lexington for a proper burial. His severed arm was about to be tossed onto the body part trash pile when Jackson's chaplain, Reverend Tucker Lacy, wrapped the arm in a blanket. He carried it to his family cemetery at Ellwood Manor, not far from the field hospital, where it was given a standard Christian burial. Reverend Lacy placed a marker on the grave as well.

Jackson's widow made it clear that she did not want her husband's arm removed from Ellwood Manor. However, in 1864, Union soldiers exhumed Jackson's arm and reburied it. In 1903, a granite stone was placed in the small cemetery by one of Jackson's former staff officers, bearing the inscription "Arm of Stonewall Jackson May 3, 1863." According to park historian Frank O'Reilly, though, no one knows for sure where Jackson's arm is really buried: "The safe thing for us to say here is that Jackson's arm was indeed buried there. It may very well have disintegrated as a result of time, being dug up and aerated—or it just simply is somewhere else in the cemetery, long lost, forgotten." So far, the park has expressed no interest in disturbing the burial site.

MISS BAKER'S SPACE CENTER GRAVE

Huntsville, Alabama

Animals were first launched into space in the early 1950s. In 1951, the United States began firing aerobic rockets containing monkeys and mice thousands of feet above the earth. On July 22, 1951, the Soviet Union successfully sent two dogs into suborbital space flight to an altitude of 331,000 feet. None of these animal astronauts, however, achieved the fame of the squirrel monkey known as "Miss Baker."

Born in Iquitos, Peru, in 1957, Miss Baker was part of a lot of twenty-five monkeys purchased from a pet shop in Miami, Florida. The monkeys were transported to the Naval Aviation Medical School in Pensacola, where they were tested for the qualifications as "monkeynauts." After being subjected to hours of confinement in small spaces and electrodes pasted all over her body, Miss Baker was selected from the fourteen suitable candidates, largely because of her intelligence and docility. She seemed to really enjoy being gently handled by the researchers, earning her the nickname "TLC" (tender loving care).

On May 28, 1959, Miss Baker was outfitted with a jacket and a helmet lined with rubber and chamois leather. A respiration meter was attached to her nose. She was placed in a shoebox-sized capsule ($9\frac{3}{4}$x$12\frac{1}{2}$x$6\frac{3}{4}$) insulated with fiberglass and rubber. Miss Baker was also equipped with an oxygen bottle with a pressure valve. At 2:30 a.m., Miss Baker and another squirrel monkey named Miss Able were launched in a Jupiter rocket from a pad in Cape Canaveral to a height of 300 miles. The sixteen-minute flight included nine minutes of weightlessness. After traveling 1,500 miles, the capsule landed in the Atlantic Ocean near Puerto Rico and was recovered by the USS *Kiowa*. Amazingly, the space monkeys had withstood the force of thirty-eight times the pull of gravity. The rescue crew also retrieved a collection of biological samples from the capsule, including samples of human blood, onions, mustard, corn seeds, yeast and sea urchin eggs and sperm.

The grave site of the space monkey named "Miss Baker" is located just outside the U.S. Space and Rocket Center at 3371.1 Tranquility Base in Huntsville, Alabama. *James E. Scarborough.*

Miss Able and Miss Baker became instant celebrities following their return to earth. A photograph of both monkeys was featured on the cover of *Life* magazine on June 15, 1959. Sadly, Miss Able died four days after the capsule was taken aboard the USS *Kiowa* from cardiac fibrillation produced by the anesthesia she was given to make it easier for researchers to remove the electrodes. Miss Baker was in the news once again in 1962 when she was married to a squirrel monkey named Big George. She remained in the Naval Aerospace Medical Center in Pensacola until 1971, when she was moved to the U.S. Rocket and Space Center in Huntsville, Alabama. She soon became a popular attraction, entertaining museum visitors. Miss Baker's next big public event was her twentieth birthday party, which was celebrated with balloons and cottage cheese, Miss Baker's favorite snack. Her birthday was celebrated every year on May 28, the date of her space launch. Her marriage to her second husband, Norman, was presided over by Alabama District Court judge Dan McCoy. On the twenty-fifth anniversary of the flight Miss Baker was given a rubber ducky and gelatin with bananas. Shortly after breaking the record for being the oldest living squirrel monkey, Miss Baker died of kidney failure at Auburn University in 1984.

Miss Baker's grave is located in a clump of trees next to the entrance of the mausoleum. She is buried next to Big George. The inscription carved on her tombstone memorializes Miss Baker's contribution to the space race:

> *Miss Baker*
> *Squirrel Monkey*
> *Born 1957*
> *First U.S. Animal*
> *To Fly in Space*
> *And Return Alive*
> *May 28, 1959*

Visitors to the grave site might find bananas placed on top of her tombstone by one of her countless fans.

THE GRAVE OF THE LADY IN RED

Cruger, Mississippi

In 1969, a work crew was using a backhoe to dig a septic tank line at Egypt Plantation in Cruger, Mississippi, when it hit something metallic three feet under the ground. Using shovels, the workers uncovered a cast-iron coffin with a glass window. Clearly visible was a woman in her twenties or thirties. She had bright auburn hair and pale white skin. She was wearing a red dress with white gloves and square-toed boots. A description of the coffin appeared in the *Clarion Ledger* (Jackson, MS), on August 29, 1969:

The method of preservation used for the Lady in Red was common prior to the Civil War, when custom-made caskets, shaped to the body, were ordered as one would order a dress. The glass that sealed the coffin was placed over the body, and alcohol was poured inside until it was level full and then sealed with a castiron tip. When the back hoe machine hit the coffin, alcohol spilled from the casket, and spots of the liquid were seen on the woman's dress.

This type of casket—the Fink Iron Caset—was popular because it enabled corpses to be transported over long distances and be viewed during the funeral. The coffin was air-tight, so there was no real danger of contagion.

The discovery of the cast-iron coffin raised a number of questions. Why was she buried in an area where there were no houses? The biggest question, of course, pertains to her identity. According to historians, the style of the woman's dress predates the Civil War. Some locals believe that she died while traveling on a paddleboat. One local historian speculated that the coffin might have fallen off a wagon and been hastily buried in a shallow grave. When she was reburied in Odd Fellows Cemetery, the birth date on her grave marker was estimated as 1835—her death date was listed as 1969. For a while, her grave site became a tourist attraction.

Jim Thomas, part owner of Egypt Plantation, has been trying to uncover the Red Lady's identity for years. "I researched to find the section where the Lady in Red was found," Thomas said. "The chain of titles goes back to 1835." He is even plannng to hire an attorney, if necessary, to find out who she is. "She has no one to speak for her," Thomas said. "She has no one to put flowers on her grave. I don't want her to ever be forgotten again."

THE GYPSY QUEEN OF ROSE HILL CEMETERY

Meridian, Mississippi

On January 31, 1915, the Queen of the Gypsy Nation, Kelly Mitchell, died in Coatopa, Alabama, while trying to give birth to her fourteenth or fifteenth child. Mitchell was forty-seven years old at the time. Her body was taken to nearby Meridian, Mississippi, because the city was said to have a refrigerated morgue. Her immediate family realized that it would be necessary to preserve her corpse at Watkins Funeral Home to allow the mourners time to travel

Since Kelly Mitchell's death on January 31, 1915, visitors to Rose Hill Cemetery have placed offerings on her grave in the hope of having their wishes granted. *Marilyn Brown.*

to the grave site from all over the country. Six weeks after Mitchell's death, four bands of gypsies attended her funeral at St. Paul's Episcopal Church: the Mitchell, Marks, Bimbo and Costello bands. Because the church was unable to accommodate all of the twenty thousand mourners, most of them gathered in small groups outside. Music for the funeral march was provided by a local college band. Walton W. Moore, tour guide at Rose Hill Cemetery, told reporter Jennifer Jacob that the mourners encouraged the band to "snap it up" because the funeral march was too slow. Kelly Mitchell was buried in Rose Hill Cemetery. Twenty-seven years later, her husband, Emil, was buried beside her.

A number of myths are associated with Kelly Mitchell's grave. Some people believe that the coffin was made of gold, even though records show that no coffin over $150 was purchased in Meridian in 1915. Some people believe that if visitors place trinkets or coins on her grave, she will express her gratitude by appearing to them in a dream and granting their wishes. It is also said that Kelly's or her husband's spirit will curse anyone who removes any of the coins or objects from their grave. Rumors that the mourners tossed twenty gold pieces into her coffin or that Kelly Mitchell was buried with her jewelry were responsible for three attempts to break into her grave, one of which resulted in the cracking of the wolf stone, which is a marble tablet placed on top of the grave.

Today, Kelly Mitchell's grave is one of Meridian's most popular tourist attractions. The fact that many of the legends surrounding her grave have been debunked has not stopped people from placing soda cans, packs of cigarettes, Mardi Gras beads and coins on the Mitchells' graves. Indeed, Meridian's indelible link to Kelly Mitchell has led some to speculate that she is the inspiration for Meridian's nickname: "The Queen City."

6

CIVIL WAR LEGENDS

CHICKAMAUGA, A LEGENDARY BATTLEFIELD

Chickamauga, Georgia

Chickamauga was the largest battle fought in the western theater and was second only to Gettysburg in the total number of casualties. It was also the first major battle fought in Georgia. On August 16, 1863, the Army of the Cumberland under the command of Major General William Starke Rosencrans began moving from middle Tennessee to the Tennessee River. By the first of September, Rosencrans had crossed the mountains of the Cumberland Plateau and was only forty miles south of Chattanooga. On September 8, the commander of the Confederate Army of Tennessee, General Braxton Bragg, abandoned Chattanooga and headed south, thereby allowing the Union army to occupy the city. Determined to retake Chattanooga, Bragg marched north and engaged the XXI Corps in battle on September 18. The next day, Bragg tried unsuccessfully to break through the Union line. On September 20, Bragg's renewed assault on the Federals was bolstered by a breakdown in communications. General Rosencrans was told, incorrectly, that a gap had formed in his line. The general's attempt to bridge the gap by moving his troops inadvertently created an actual gap. Taking advantage of Rosencrans's tactical blunder, Confederate lieutenant general James Longstreet moved the eight brigades under his command through the gap, forcing one-third of the Union forces off the field.

The battle would have ended with a complete rout of the Union army had not Major General George H. Thomas formed a defensive line at Snodgrass Hill. Despite Bragg's repeated assaults against the Union army, the line held firm. At twilight, the Union forces returned to Chattanooga to await further attacks by Confederate troops from the surrounding heights. By battle's end, Rosencrans's losses totaled 16,170; Bragg's losses totaled 18,454. Among those killed on the Confederate side was Benjamin Hardin Helm, the brother of President Abraham Lincoln's wife, Mary.

Not surprisingly, Chickamauga is one of the most haunted Civil War battlefields in the United States. One of these spirits had close ties to the battle's bloody aftermath. After the armies relocated to Chattanooga, the hills and fields of Chickamauga were littered with the detritus of war: shattered caissons, broken cannon, rifles, canteens, shell fragments and the mangled bodies of horses and men. Many of the Union soldiers lay where they fell for two months before they were finally given a decent burial. For many days, local women wandered through the battlefield with their lanterns searching for friends and loved ones. The lucky ones discovered their soldiers recovering in one of the area's many field hospitals. Others found the mangled corpses of their husbands, brothers or lovers lying in secluded spots. People say that the wailing of these women echoed through the battlefield day and night. Reed Bridge is named after one of these women, Abigail Reed, who found the corpse of the young Confederate soldier she was engaged to and buried him where he lay. Tragically, 1,500 Confederates and 5,000 Federals were missing in action. A female specter known as "The Lady in White" is said to be the ghost of a young woman who continued searching for her beau years after the battle end. After the deranged woman's death, she was buried in her white wedding gown. Her mournful apparition has been sighted for many years by tourists from all over the world, many of whom were unfamiliar with the legend. She is said to disappear when witnesses come too close.

Chickamauga's most famous ghost is a terrifying entity known as "Old Green Eyes." According to the oldest origin story, this demonic figure may have been responsible for the complete disappearance of a nameless tribe who hunted at Chickamauga before the Cherokee arrived. Some witnesses swore that they sighted this terrifying creature prowling around during the battle. However, many people believe that "Old Green Eyes" is the apparition of a soldier who was blown to pieces by a cannonball during the battle. He may be the ghost of a soldier under General Resencrans's command named Colonel Julius Garesche, who was killed by a cannonball. Some witnesses describe him as a disembodied head with glowing green

The heroic stand made by the 125th Ohio Volunteer Regiment under the command of Colonel Emerson Opdycke is memorialized by this striking monument at Chickamauga Battlefield. "Opdycke's Tigers," as the regiment is known, is represented by this stone tiger, which, some say, prowls around at night. *Alan Brown.*

eyes that hovers approximately six feet off the ground. In 1999, a visitor who had been walking around the battlefield all day was distracted by a long, sustained moan coming from the woods. Concerned that someone might have been injured, he took several steps toward the woods. Suddenly, a head with phosphorescent eyes floated out from between the trees in his directions. The young man immediately turned around and ran as fast as he could to his car. As he sailed out of the park, he said he was too frightened to even look back. Some people say they have seen a headless apparition combing the battlefield for its head. Many employees and visitors believe that "Old Green Eyes" has the ability to change his shape. In 1976, a former chief ranger was walking down Kelly Road when he saw a six-foot-tall man-like figure walking in his direction. As the weird man came closer, the former ranger could tell that he has long, stringy hair, orange-green eyes and pointed teeth.

The legend of "Old Green Eyes" may have been spawned by the Opdyke monument on Snodgrass Hill, which commemorates the feats of the 125th Ohio Volunteers, also known as the Tiger Regiment. As the Confederate forces poured through the gap in the Federal lines on September 20, Opdyke's unit of one thousand men regrouped on Snodgrass Hill in a last-ditch effort to halt Longstreet's advancing troops. Seventeen of the 125th Ohio Volunteers perished, eighty-three were wounded and five were lost. The sculpted image of a ferocious tiger standing atop the monument symbolizes the brave efforts of Opdyke's unit to achieve the impossible. Some people believe that "Old Green Eyes" is actually the spectral form of Opdyke's tiger, which prowls the park late at night. In 1980, a seventeen-year-old employee of Krystal's in Fort Oglethorpe was driving home through the park late one night when she beheld what she described as a green-eyed panther on the S-curve about twenty feet away from her car. She drove away from the creature as fast as she could.

Another monument to the Union army is Wilder Tower. It was erected in 1902 to memorialize the valiant but failed attempt by mounted infantrymen from Illinois and Indiana to stand against Longstreet's army just south of Snodgrass Hill. The tower itself is not believed to be haunted, even though a number of suicides have taken place in or around it. However, strange events have occurred near the tower. In 1990, a group of teenagers were on a hayride near Wilder Tower in 1990 when they heard the hoof beats of a horse riding toward them. The rider appeared to be holding a flaming torch. As the rider neared the hay wagon, the riders could make out the figure of a skeleton in a ragged uniform holding a torch. The rider disappeared as he attempted to climb down from his horse.

Not far from Wilder Tower is a row of monuments, one of which is the Wisconsin Cavalry Monument. In her book *Ghosts of the Southern Tennessee Valley*, Georgiana C. Kotarski writes that the widow of an officer killed during the battle gave two emeralds from her earrings to the sculptor to be used as the eyes of "the Riderless Horse," as the monument has come to be

Wilder Tower is an eighty-five-foot memorial to Colonel John T. Wilder's "Lightning Brigade," composed of regiments from Illinois and Indiana. *Alan Brown.*

known. When the statue was unveiled the next morning, the emeralds were gone. The rumor soon spread that the ghost of the woman's husband had taken the emeralds and that he walks through the battlefield looking for her.

Most of the nighttime paranormal activity on the battlefield cannot be traced to a single individual. For years, people have seen balls of light flitting over the hills and through the woods. A couple of eyewitnesses swore that when they approached the orbs, they turned into a dark, humanoid shape that vanished in a few seconds. A group of living history reenactors sighted a strange orange light that trailed them as they walked on a dirt road in the Environmental Study Area. One theory holds that these "ghost lights" are made by the lanterns held by the ghost of women who still patrol the battlefield in search of their loved ones. The screams of dying horses and soldiers still resonate through the hills. Some claim to have heard sounds of rifles and cannon fire that appear to be near and distant at the same time. For many of the men who died at Chickamauga, the battle rages on.

THE GHOSTS OF LOOKOUT MOUNTAIN

Chattanooga, Tennessee

Lookout Mountain rises 1,700 feet above the city of Chattanooga. For centuries, its three almost vertical sides have given the defenders of the city a formidable defensive position from invaders. Lookout Mountain is also known for a weather phenomenon that adds to its mysterious aura. Three or four times a year, a cloud bank forms at the base and, within a few hours, envelops the entire mountain. This weather anomaly formed the backdrop of what has come to be known as "The Battle Above the Clouds."

Following the Confederate victory at Chickamauga, General Braxton Bragg's army positioned itself at the top of Lookout Mountain. On November 23, 1863, Union general George H. Thomas's men overran the Confederate units at Orchard Knob, causing General Braxton Bragg to move General William T. Walker's division from the base of Lookout Mountain to Missionary Ridge. As a result, Confederate general Carter Stevenson was left with only two brigades to defend the Cravens House at the top of the mountain. Despite the mountain's formidable terrain, General Ulysses S. Grant ordered General Joseph Hooker to move his three divisions against the Confederate left on November 24. Hooker's troops moved along the base of the mountain to the point that had been weakened by Walker's removal the night before. The Mississippi brigade under the command of General Edward Walthall attempted unsuccessfully to thwart the advance of Federal troops at the Cravens House. A regiment of Union soldiers, many of whom had been wounded in the conflict, wandered over to the eastern side of Lookout Mountain on their way back

Three or four times a year, a cloud bank forms at the base and eventually envelops all of Lookout Mountain, just as it did during the battle. *Alan Brown.*

On November 24, 1863, Union forces under Major General Joseph Hooker defeated Confederate forces commanded by Major General Carter L. Stevenson, who placed an artillery battery on the crest of Lookout Mountain. *Alan Brown.*

Robert Cravens's home on top of Lookout Mountain was used as headquarters and as an observation point by the Union and Confederate armies. *Alan Brown.*

north. Within the next few months, many of them were shot and killed by locals. A small band of seven of the surviving soldiers was last seen in Blanche, Alabama. In his book *Ghosts of Lookout Mountain*, Larry Hillhouse wrote that on rainy, overcast days, locals have heard the cries and curses of dying men and the spectral sound of marching feet. Some people have found footprints that start in the middle of nowhere and extend a few hundred yards into a field near the mountain. Apparently, the ghosts of the lost regiment are still trying to find their way home.

Hillhouse tells another story about one of Lookout Mountain's many scenic overlooks that were used by both the Confederate and Union armies to track the movement of enemy forces. One of the more secluded overlooks provided an excellent view of the eastern side of the mountain. After the Federals took control of Chattanooga and the surrounding area, a Confederate sentry who was sick and wounded remained hidden in the overlook for several weeks until finally succumbing to starvation. Locals claim that the ghost of the dedicated soldier is still at his post, sending messages to his comrades by means of smoke signals and flashes of light from a pocket mirror.

THE LEGEND OF THE CONFEDERATE ROCKET

Richmond, Virginia

The Civil War was a time marked by technological change. Many of these innovations were available only to Union troops because the North had the industries and skills to produce them. One example is the Spencer carbine, which instilled fear and envy in the hearts of Confederate troops because it could fire seven shots in thirty seconds. The Union army also had hydrogen-filled balloons and iron-clad warships. Necessity prompted the Confederates to produce submarines, like the CSS *Hunley,* to destroy these formidable additions to the Union fleet. The Confederates also made improvements on an eighteenth-century concept called the floating battery, which consisted of guns mounted to a floating craft. The resourcefulness of the Confederacy is undeniable. However, were the Confederates able to build and launch a two-stage missile at war's end?

The legend has its roots in a newspaper story written by a Vienna correspondent who identified himself only as "C.R. Johnson." According to Johnson, in 1865, a secret agent working for the Confederacy in London enlisted the aid of Lord Kelvin to liquefy oxygen. The Confederacy planned to construct a high-powered missile using British machinery for liquefying oxygen and a small turbine and a gyroscopic stabilizer created by German physicist Ernst Mach. The two-stage rocket was to be fired from a tube inserted in a deep hole in a riverbank. The tube, constructed at the Tredegar Iron Works in Richmond, was pieced together from the barrels of naval guns. Gun-cotton ignited at the bottom of the tube supplied the rocket's thrust. In early March 1865, the missile was transported through the streets of Richmond to the launching site. Power for the rocket's stabilizing vanes was provided through a steam pipe that fed into the launching tube. The letters *CSA* were cut into the missile's nose; President Jefferson Davis and other high-ranking officials are said to have added their names to the missile.

Just before the launch, a squadron of scouts was dispatched between Richmond and Washington to serve as rudimentary tracking station outposts. When the missile was fired by means of electrical switches, a number of observers using telescopes watched the missile soar into the heavens. Almost as soon as the missile jettisoned its first stage, it vanished from sight. No one saw the missile return to earth. The first stage, however, was recovered and stored away in a torpedo shed. Because official records were destroyed in the fall of Richmond, no proof of the rocket's existence has survived.

C.R. Johnson asserted that the son of a Confederate spy in Britain was in possession of official documentation of the launch, but he was reluctant to endure the public attention that would accompany their public release.

This amazing story is difficult to accept at face value in the absence of proof. In 2005, *MythBusters* put this legend to the test. Using only materials that would have been available to engineers during the Civil War, Jamie and Adam constructed and launched a one-stage hybrid rocket. Because the missile traveled only five hundred yards, the team concluded that it would have been impossible for the Confederacy to build a rocket on the scale described in Johnson's newspaper story. So, is the story of the Confederate rocket nothing more than a hoax perpetrated by an imaginative journalist? Or, has an ancient rocket bearing the insignia *CSA* been orbiting the earth for over a century?

THE DRUMMER BOY OF SHILOH

Shiloh National Battlefield, Tennessee

The Civil War has been called "The Boys' War," primarily because so many teenagers fought and died on the battlefield. Although young men had to be eighteen to enlist in the Union army, many of them were younger because they lied about their age. However, drummer boys were vitally important to the war effort, even though they were not allowed to fire guns. Because it was difficult to hear the commands of officers over the din of battle, drummer boys were given a series of beats that signified specific orders, such as "attack now," "meet here" and "retreat." After the battle, many drummer boys were used as stretcher bearers. They were sent out to search for wounded soldiers and carry them back to the field hospital. Undoubtedly, the most famous of these brave youngsters was Johnny Clem, "The Drummer Boy of Shiloh."

Johnny Clem was born in Newark, Ohio, on August 13, 1851. He ran away from home in May 1861 at age nine to join the Union army. He drilled with the Third Ohio Volunteer Infantry Regiment for a while, but the commander rejected him because he "wasn't enlisting infants." When the Twenty-Second Michigan Infantry Regiment marched through Newark, Clem tried once again to enlist. When told that he was too young, he tagged along behind the regiment until finally wearing down the officer in charge. He could not join the army officially, but he was allowed to perform camp

Gen. Clem the Drummer boy of Shiloh
Picture made at the age of 12 (1863)

Ten-year-old John Clem is said to have served as mascot and drummer boy in the Twenty-Second Michigan Volunteer Infantry during the Battle of Shiloh. *Heritage Auctions*.

duties and to draw a soldier's pay of thirteen dollars a month, most of which was donated by the officers. His fellow soldiers took him under their wing, giving him a small gun and uniform and training him to be a drummer.

Soldiers began speaking of Clem's courage under fire in April 1861 during the Battle of Shiloh. Supposedly, his drum was smashed by a Confederate cannonball while he was beating it. He was allowed to enlist in the U.S. Army in May 1863. In September 1863 at the Battle of Chickamauga, Clem was wielding his little rifle and riding a caisson. When General William Rosecrans's Army of the Cumberland was in full retreat, a Confederate officer is said to have run up to Clem and exclaim, "Surrender, you damned little Yankee!" Clem promptly shot and killed him.

Some aspects of Johnny Clem's military career have been called into question. Although Clem actually did fight at Chickamauga, Clem's unit, the Twenty-Second Michigan, was not mustered until the summer following the Battle of Shiloh. While Clem could have possibly fought with a different unit at the Battle of Shiloh, some scholars contend that the U.S. Army may have exaggerated some of Clem's exploits for propaganda purposes.

Clem participated in several other battles in the Civil War, including Murfreesboro, Perryville, Kennesaw and Atlanta. By the time he was discharged from the army in 1864 at age thirteen, Clem had been wounded twice. After the war, President Ulysses S. Grant nominated Clem for admission at the United States Military Academy at West Point. Clem failed the entrance exam several times, but Grant appointed him a second lieutenant anyway. He eventually became a colonel and assistant quartermaster general. When he retired as a brigadier general in 1915, Clem was the last Civil War veteran to leave the military. Clem died in San Antonio, Texas, in 1937. He is buried at Arlington National Cemetery.

THE ANGEL OF MARYE'S HEIGHTS

Fredericksburg, Virginia

The Battle of Fredericksburg is notable, not only because it was one of the earliest battles, but also because more men fought in this battle—nearly 200,000—than in any other in the entire war between December 11 and 15, 1862. Determined to bring the war to a rapid conclusion by taking Richmond, Virginia, Major General Ambrose E. Burnside moved his troops to the city of Falmouth opposite Fredericksburg. General Robert E. Lee responded to Burnside's aggressive actions by positioning his army on the heights above Fredericksburg. Burnside, however, was unable to cross the Rappahannock River to Fredericksburg for two weeks while awaiting the arrival of his pontoon bridges. Five bridges were laid on December 11, and over 100,000 Federal soldiers began crossing the river the next day. On December 13, Burnside attacked Prospect Hill and Marye's Heights, resulting in tremendous losses. An attempt by Major General George G. Meade's division to break through General "Stonewall" Jackson's line was repelled. On December 15, Burnside's army retreated across the river, giving Lee one of his greatest victories. Over 13,000 Union soldiers were killed in the battle, compared to 5,000 Confederate casualties. The most celebrated hero of this bloody battle was, ironically, a man who risked his life delivering aid to the enemy.

Richard Bowland Kirkland was born on a farm near Flat Rock, South Carolina, in 1843. Kirkland's mother died when he was two years old, so he was raised by his father, who had four other boys and a daughter to take care of as well. He was a religious boy who attended Flat Rock Baptist Church. Instead of being taught the Three Rs, Kirkland learned how to shoot and how to care for and ride horses. By the time war was declared in 1861, he stood five feet, eight inches tall and weighed 150 pounds. He was a handsome, strapping young man with a thin face, dark hair and a moustache. He enlisted in the Confederate army in 1861; by 1862, Kirkland had been promoted to the rank of sergeant in Company G, Second South Carolina Infantry.

On December 13, 1862, stretcher bearers were doing their best to remove the hundreds of Union soldiers who had fallen in a failed attempt to breach the stone wall behind which Confederate forces were unleashing their "sheet of flame" at the base of Marye's Heights. The Confederate soldiers crouching on the other side of the wall listened silently to the cries of enemy soldiers, pleading with anyone to bring them water. Finally, one Confederate soldier, Richard Kirkland, could stand hearing the pleas of the dying men just outside the wall no longer. He ran over to the Stevens House, which General Joseph B. Kershaw was using as his headquarters, and asked for permission to fill his canteens with water and give it to the Union soldiers. Kershaw told Kirkland that he could not allow him to use his white handkerchief as a flag of truce, but he gave the young man permission to climb over the wall and tend to the dying men. With several canteens slung over his shoulder, Kirkland climbed over the wall and approached the nearest soldier. He then proceeded to lay the man's knapsack under the man's head and pour water into his open mouth. In his account of the incident published in the *Charleston News and Courier* in January 1880 and later in the *New York Times*, Kershaw wrote,

> *By this time, his purpose was well understood on both sides, and all danger was over. From all parts of the field arose fresh cries of "Water, God's sake, water!"…For an hour and a half did this ministering angel pursue his labor of mercy, nor ceased to go and return until he had relieved all of the wounded on that part of the field. He returned wholly unhurt.*

Richard Kirkland was killed at the Battle of Chickamauga. However, Kirkland's unselfish act during the Battle of Fredericksburg lived on after him. Around the turn of the century, an artist named William Ludwell Sheppard immortalized the sergeant's compassionate acts in a stirring painting. In 1908, Walter Clark wrote a poem memorializing Richard Kirkland. In 1965, Dr. Richard Nunn Lanier led a petition to the state legislatures of South Carolina and Virginia to erect a bronze monument to "The Angel of Marye's Heights" at the northeast corner of Sunken Road and Mercer Street.

No one really doubted the story of "The Angel of Marye's Heights" until the twenty-first century, when historians began taking a close look at the details. Some historians claim that it is impossible to determine if it actually was Kirkland who gave water to the Union soldiers. Others have asserted that even if this incident really did occur, the Confederate soldier probably had no more than a few minutes to do the job. Also, only a few of the thousands of soldiers who were on the battlefield at the time offered corroborating evidence. One of these eyewitnesses was a colonel with the First South Carolina who said that one of his men really did bring water to wounded soldiers over the wall. A captain with the Third South Carolina, August Dickert, said that a Georgia soldier performed the deed. The poet Walt Whitman, who worked as a nurse at a Washington hospital during the Civil War, reported that a soldier who had been wounded at Fredericksburg told him that "a middle-aged man" crossed the line and gave water to his comrades. These accounts run counter to the testimony from Kirkland's fellow soldiers given after the publication of Kershaw's article in 1880 that he really did minister to the needs of his foes on December 13, 1863. Most of these soldiers claimed that Kirkland was cheered on by Union and Confederate soldiers alike, although a few swore that bullets were whizzing by the man's head as he bent down to give the wounded a drink of water. Until indisputable proof of Kirkland's deeds surfaces, the story of "The Angel of Marye's Heights" will be viewed by skeptics as an inspirational, but probably apocryphal, tale.

THE SWORD IN THE TREE, A TRUE STORY?

Birmingham, Alabama

Arlington is an antebellum home located on six acres at 331 Cotton Avenue SW in the Arlington–West End neighborhood of Birmingham. The mansion's history can be traced back to Stephen Hall's purchase of 4.75 acres from William O. Tarrant and John Burford. Dr. Hall and his family started out living in a log cabin he built on the property. As time passed, he enlarged the home to two stories with four rooms. Following Hall's death, Samuel Mudd purchased the house in 1842. He replaced Hall's modest home with a much larger one he called "The Grove." His new house was an eight-room mansion built in the Greek Revival style. He then entered the world of politics and law. He served in the Alabama legislature from 1843 to 1848. Mudd was elected circuit judge in 1856, and he held that position until 1883. Mudd's house was spared the destruction of the Civil War when General James H. Wilson used it as his temporary headquarters in the spring of 1865.

After Mudd died in 1884, the property went through several owners. In 1902, the owner of the Continental Gin Company, Robert Munger, bought the house and property. He promptly changed the name of the home to "Arlington" in honor of Robert E. Lee's estate. Munger divided up the property among his children. The main house, Arlington, was passed down to his daughter, Ruby, and her husband, Alexander Montgomery. Arlington remained in the Montgomery family for thirty years until it was put up for sale in 1952. Morgan Smith chaired a committee to raise money to transform the old house into a museum. The house was finally purchased for $53,000 in 1953. The Arlington Historical Association assumed the task of restoring and furnishing the house.

Arlington was built at 331 Cotton Avenue SW in Birmingham, Alabama, between 1845 and 1850. *Library of Congress, Prints & Photographs Division, AL-424.*

An important element of Arlington's romantic allure is the Civil War legend for which it is famous. The story goes that in 1861, Samuel Mudd's daughter, Molly, was saying goodbye to her sweetheart, Robert Earle, on the front lawn of his family home. Before riding off, Earle drove his sword into a nearby oak tree and vowed to remove it when he returned. For months, Molly thought of Robert every time she gazed at the sword protruding from the trunk of the tree. One fateful day, Molly received word that Robert had been killed in battle. For the rest of her life, she thought of Robert's presence every time she passed by the tree and gazed at the sword. The sword remained in the tree well into the twentieth century.

Unlike many romantic legends, this one has a kernel of truth. When this author visited Arlington in 2008, he learned that the sword was actually a scythe. Over time, the handle of the scythe rotted off, and the tree grew around the blade. In the 1960s, the tree was removed during the construction of an apartment, and the chunk of wood containing the blade was taken to Arlington. It was thought lost for quite a while until the director discovered it lying on top of a secretary when the house was being remodeled. It is now on display inside the house. Apparently, the relic has attracted the attention of Molly Mudd's spirit, which is credited with slamming doors and rocking chairs by way of making its presence known.

7

MYSTERIOUS PEOPLE

JOHN ST. HELEN'S TRUE IDENTITY

Granbury, Texas

The death of John Wilkes Booth is part of the historic record. After shooting President Abraham Lincoln at Ford's Theatre on April 14, 1865, Booth jumped from the box shouting "Sic semper tyrannis!" Even though he broke his leg in the fall, Booth was able to mount his horse and ride out of town with an accomplice, David Herold. In the hours that followed, over one thousand Union soldiers combed the countryside for the assassin and his fellow conspirators. With the help of confederate sympathizers, Booth and Herold were able to cross the Potomac and Rappahannock Rivers into Virginia. On the morning of April 26, Union troops surrounded the tobacco barn on Richard Garrett's farm where Booth and Herold were sleeping. Herold surrendered, but Booth fired back. The soldiers set fire to the barn in an attempt to flush Booth out. As he staggered out of the barn, Booth was shot in the neck by Boston Corbett. He died a few hours later on the porch of the Garretts' home. John Wilkes Booth was secretly buried in Washington, D.C.'s Old Penitentiary, but in 1869, his body was exhumed and interred in an unmarked grave in the Booth family plot at Green Mount Cemetery in Baltimore, Maryland. This is the official version of the death of John Wilkes Booth. The citizens of Granbury, Texas, beg to differ.

According to the local legend, high-ranking officials in Lincoln's administration helped John Wilkes Booth escape; Booth fled to Glen Rose, Texas, where he set up a store on the grounds of a mill. The night a U.S. marshal arrived in Glen Rose to marry a local girl, Booth left and moved to Granbury sometime in the 1870s. He tended bar under the name John St. Helen at a saloon that has been converted into a gift shop. Stories passed down from people who knew John St. Helen reveal that he walked with a limp and bore an uncanny resemblance to Lincoln's assassin. They also said that he acted occasionally at the opera house. Although St. Helen was around liquor every day, his closest friend, a lawyer named Finis L. Bates, said that he never took a drop until April 14—the anniversary of the assassination of Abraham Lincoln. On that particular day, he got "roaring drunk."

The story goes that one day, St. Helen became very sick while living in Granbury. When the local doctor informed St. Helen that there was nothing he could do for him, he asked Bates to come to his bedside and hear his deathbed confession: "My name is not John St. Helen. I am John Wilkes Booth, the assassin of Abraham Lincoln." Despite the doctor's fatal diagnosis of St. Helen's illness, he eventually recovered and left Granbury. No one in town, including Bates, ever heard from him again.

Finis Bates claimed to have encountered St. Helen once more in 1906 in Enid, Oklahoma. A homeless alcoholic named David George confessed on his deathbed that he was John Wilkes Booth. Bates examined the corpse. Even in the face ravaged by hard living and hard drinking, the image of Bates's old friend John St. Helen was evident. Bates claimed the corpse and had it embalmed.

The mummified corpse remained in Bates's possession for a number of years. Sometime in the next decade, the mummy was taken by someone else and displayed as a sideshow attraction in carnivals, circuses and sideshows throughout the 1920s and into the 1960s. It was billed as "The Corpse of John Wilkes Booth, the Assassin of Abraham Lincoln." X-rays revealed that the man's left ankle had been broken and poorly set. Photographs of the mummy indicated that the preservation process caused it to turn completely black. The mummy itself has disappeared, so DNA testing is impossible. Booth's family has refused to allow DNA testing to be performed on Booth's corpse. Consequently, the riddle of John St. Helen's true identity may never be solved.

THE CURSE OF ANNIE MITCHELL

Mount Sterling, Kentucky

Annie Mitchell was a dark-haired beauty who was hailed as the "belle of Central Kentucky" in the mid-nineteenth century. In her late teens, she had her choice of suitors from wealthy families, but she fell in love with a tall, blond young man named John Bell Hood, who lived not far from the Mitchell home. Hood began courting her in 1849 while on furlough from West Point. The couple spent long evenings walking in the garden of Hood's family home. Their budding romance was short-lived, however; Annie's family pressured her to marry a young man from a wealthy family who is remembered today as "Mr. Anderson." She agreed to marry Anderson, on the condition that she be allowed to write Hood a letter. In her letter, she broke off her romance with Hood but assured him that she would "love him forever." When the cadet received the letter, he jumped on his horse and rode back to Kentucky. Hood managed to send a message to Annie asking her to meet him a few nights later at a spot near her house so that they could ride off and get married. Annie left the house at the appointed time, but one of the slaves noted her absence and alerted her father. Hood was lifting Annie Mitchell onto the saddle of his horse when her father and brother rode up and brought her home. She was locked in her room until she agreed to marry Anderson. After several days, Annie finally consented to marry a man she did not love.

A few months later, Annie married her parents' choice for a husband. For the next few months, Annie never left her room in the Mitchell house. When she discovered she was pregnant, she refused to speak. Even Anderson was not allowed to visit her in her room. After her son Corwin was born, she delivered a curse "upon all who had any part in making me marry Anderson when my heart will always belong to John Bell Hood." Legend has it that the curse began taking effect soon after she uttered it. Only a few hours after Corwin was born, a severe thunderstorm built up. As wind and rain pummeled the area, a lightning bolt struck the corner of the Mitchell house, causing one of the walls of the house to collapse. Three members of the Mitchell household were killed: the brother who had prevented her from riding off with Hood, the slave girl who raised the alarm when Annie tried to sneak out of the house and Annie herself.

Soon, news of Annie's curse spread throughout the county. Over the next few years, people spoke of the curse when tragedy befell her family. Corwin's son, English Anderson, was an angry young man who was given to violent outbursts. One day, he threw a brick at his younger brother and knocked him off his horse. When Corwin learned of the boy's injury, he staggered into his bedroom and died of a heart attack. The youngest son died of his injures just a few hours later. Not long thereafter, English Anderson was stoned to death by a mob after stabbing a man and beating a boy to death who worked on his farm. The family curse persisted in the 1940s when Annie's great-grandson Judson shot himself in the head while standing in a pond. Ironically, Annie's ghost appears as a benevolent spirt who walks through the gardens in the Hood home, just as she did when John Bell Hood was courting her.

Some people believe that the direct effects of Annie Mitchell's curse were somehow passed on to John Bell Hood. His career had a promising start. During the Civil War, he distinguished himself as commander of the Texas Brigade. He lost an arm and a leg in the fighting at Chickamauga but rose to the rank of general at the age of thirty-three. However, his Army of Tennessee was driven out of Atlanta in 1864 and was annihilated at the Battle of Nashville. After the war, he went bankrupt and died, along with his wife, in New Orleans's yellow fever epidemic of 1879.

VIRGINIA'S JACK THE RIPPER

Norfolk, Virginia

Born in Liverpool, Merseyside, on October 24, 1838, James Maybrick was the son of an engraver named William Maybrick and his wife, Susanna. As an adult, Maybrick worked in Liverpool as a cotton merchant. He frequently traveled to the United States on business trips before establishing a branch office in Norfolk, Virginia, in 1871. Three years later, Maybrick contracted malaria and became one of thousands of men who was addicted to arsenic, the component of a popular treatment for malaria at that time. While traveling aboard a ship headed back to London on March 12, 1880, Maybrick met an attractive eighteen-year-old girl, Florence Elizabeth Chandler, from Mobile, Alabama. In spite of the twenty-six-year age difference, their casual relationship bloomed into a bona fide love affair. They were married on July 27, 1881, at St. James Church, Piccadilly, London. The couple lived at Maybrick's home, Battlecrease House, in Liverpool. Florence gave birth to two children: James Chandler (1882) and Gladys Evelyn (1886). Evidence suggests that Maybrick's business trips to the United States might have generated friction in their marriage. After a few years, both Maybrick and his wife began having extramarital affairs. Maybrick's health broke down completely on April 27, 1889, and he died on May 12, 1889.

The sudden onset of Maybrick's fatal illness aroused the suspicions of his brothers. An inquest conducted at a hotel determined that arsenic poising was the cause of death. Florence Maybrick was arrested several days later. She was tried at Liverpool Crown Court and found guilty of murder. The judge sentenced her to death, but irregularities in the court proceedings resulted in her sentence being commuted to life imprisonment. Her case was reexamined in 1904, and she was released. Florence Maybrick died on October 23, 1941.

The murder of James Maybrick was relegated to the status of a historical footnote until 1992. Michael Barrett, and unemployed scrap metal dealer, claimed that he had been given James Maybrick's diary by a friend, Tony Devereux, in a Liverpool pub. Although Maybrick's name does not appear in the diary, people familiar with his life history have ascribed the diary to him. In the diary, the author claims responsibility for the murders of five prostitutes in the Whitechapel district of London over several months in 1888. These are the murders that had been credited to the anonymous nineteenth-century serial killer known as Jack the Ripper. Doubt was cast on the veracity of Barrett's account from the beginning. His wife, Ann, said that the diary had been in her family since World War II. According to an electrician working in the Battlecrease House in 1992, he found the diary under the floorboards of the house and gave it to Barrett.

Barrett acquired a literary agent who arranged to have the book published under the title *The Diary of Jack the Ripper: The Chilling Confessions of James Maybrick*. The book sold well, even though some critics labeled it as a hoax. They argued that the book contained no information from the period that could not have been found in old police records. Joe Nickell found the handwriting to be consistent with that of the twentieth century, not the Victorian era. However, in 2017, researchers reported that the paper, ink and idioms used in the author's writing style date to the late Victorian period. Also, the murders officially attributed to Jack the Ripper took place in 1888, one year before Maybrick died, so he was alive at the time of the slayings. Some supporters of the authenticity of the diary suggest that Maybrick may have discovered his wife's infidelities and he took his anger out on the Whitechapel prostitutes. The true identity of Jack the Ripper will remain a mystery until definitive proof comes to light.

THE TRAGIC TALE OF FLOATING ISLAND

Mobile, Alabama

Not much is known of the woman called "Floating Island." According to her death certificate, she was born Mary Eoline Eilands in Charleston, South Carolina, on November 12, 1854. Her father, William Eilands, was a compositor for the *Mobile Press Register*. After he was promoted to the position of printer, he moved his family to several different houses in Mobile, finally settling at 655 St. Emanuel Street. Mary lived in this house until she died in 1937. By the time of her death, the neighborhood had become rundown.

She was given the name "Floating Island" because of the way she walked in her hoop skirts. She took very short steps, giving onlookers the impression that she was floating down the street. Longtime residents of Mobile recalled seeing her walking down to the docks, waiting for her seafaring lover's return. Supposedly, she was waiting for her sailor on the steps of the Cathedral of the Immaculate Conception on her wedding day when news came that he died somewhere in Mobile Bay. In another version of the legend, she received news on her wedding day that her bridegroom had been killed in battle. She continued her daily vigil for sixty-five years. Apparently, the loss of her fiancé was too much for her mind to bear.

Time stopped for her on her wedding day. She continued wearing Victorian dresses, the same ones she wore as a girl, for the remainder of her life. Every day, she said her prayers at the Cathedral of the Immaculate Conception, wearing a hat, a full black skirt, a faded white shirtwaist and low-heeled black shoes. On cold winter days, she added a rust-colored shawl to her ensemble. After saying her prayers, Mary walked over to Smith's bakery to get a piece of day-old bread. At the Florida Fish Market, she was given scrap meat and fish. She was probably supported financially by her family members until they all died off.

Over time, residents of Mobile became fearful of Floating Island. It was said to be bad luck if she crossed your path. Some ships' crews who encountered her on the way to work would turn around and go home. Some of this fear of the poor woman was justified. If she asked a passerby for money and was refused, she assailed the person with a barrage of curses until receiving what she had asked for. Some of the "bad boys" in the neighborhood threw rocks at her and her cats. The locals' fear of Floating Island could have been caused by the belief that people who have suffered misfortune in their lives tend to create more misfortune for others.

After Mary Eilands died on September 23, 1937, her funeral was held at the mortuary of Roche's Undertaking Establishment at the corner of Government and Franklin. Afterward, her body was moved to the Cathedral of the Immaculate Conception, where the priest, Monsignor S.J. Hackett, conducted a Mass for the unfortunate woman. She was buried in the Eilands plot in Magnolia Cemetery. Her grave is marked by an unmarked stone.

MAYHAYLEY LANCASTER: THE SEER OF HEARD COUNTY

Heard County, Georgia

Mayhayley Lancaster was born on October 18, 1875, in Heard County, Georgia. She had several vocations in her life, working as a schoolteacher, a newspaper reporter, a businesswoman, a door-to-door saleswoman, a farmer and a lawyer. She ran for the Georgia legislature in 1926. Even though she was defeated, several of the policy changes she advocated eventually became law, such as the construction of roads and railroads in rural counties. She achieved her greatest fame, however, as a gifted psychic.

People who knew Mayhayley Lancaster describe her as a good Christian woman who had a glass eye and wore her brother's military hat and military shirt. She lived with her pack of dogs in a cabin on a dirt road way out in the country. Her psychic powers surfaced at the age of twelve, when she began doing readings by tracing the lines in a client's hand. Some say her psychic ability to communicate with the spirits assisted her in her readings. Years later, she aided people in their searches for lost items and for missing persons. Mayhayley's fee for doing a reading was "a dollar and a dime; the dollar for me and the dime for the dogs." People who knew her said she hid the money she earned in her mattress and in chicken coops and pig pens.

Her fame as a psychic grew in 1948, when the seventy-one-year-old Mayhayley participated in the trial of John Wallace, a landowner in Coweta County who was implicated in the disappearance of Wilson Turner, a sharecropper. The sheriff, Lamar Potts, asked Mayhayley to use her psychic powers to locate the missing man. She not only revealed the location of Turner's corpse but also described the condition of the remains. Wallace was convicted on the charge of murder and executed.

Mayhayley Lancaster was a wealthy woman when she died on November 22, 1955. Her life has spawned a number of legends in the decades since her death, probably because of her affinity with the paranormal. Some residents of Heard County believe that following her death, agents of the federal government removed her head for research. Because of the desecration of her corpse, she knocked down her tombstone and laid it on her grave. Legend also has it that bad luck will follow anyone who removes objects placed on her grave by her admirers.

THE MYSTERIOUS MELUNGEONS

East Kentucky and East Tennessee

"Melungeon" is a name that has applied for centuries to the mixed-race inhabitants of the mountains of Eastern Tennessee and Eastern Kentucky. Beginning in 1654, French and English explorers traveling through the southern Appalachian Mountains reported finding dark-skinned, dark-haired people with blue eyes living in cabins and practicing Christianity. It is generally believed that the name is derived from the French word for mixture—mélange—although some scholars have traced the origin of the word back to the English word *malengin*, meaning "guile" or "deceit." No one knows for certain where the Melungeons came from originally. Some say that they are descendants of the colonists of Roanoke, who may have intermarried with local Indian tribes. N. Brent Kennedy, author of *The Melungeons: The Resurrection of a Proud People*, believes that the ancestors of the Melungeons are people of Mediterranean descent who settled in the Appalachian Mountains in 1567 and intermarried with the Creeks, Yuchis, Catawbas, Pamunkeys and Powhatans. In 1969, Eloy Gallegos took 177 DNA samples of people living in East Tennessee and found that the closest matches were from Libya, Cypress, Malta, Italy, Portugal and Spain. The possibility also exists that the Melungeons are a triracial blend of Indians, runaway American slaves and Caucasian Europeans.

Explanations for the origin of the Melungeons can be found in folklore as well. For generations, mountaineers living in East Tennessee and East Kentucky have passed down tales of shipwrecked sailors from Carthage or Phoenicians, who arrived in the New World with hoards of gold and silver. Others have theorized that the Melungeons are descended from the Welsh explorer Madoc and his crew, who, legend has it, explored the Appalachian Mountains in the 1100s. Some say that Sir Francis Drake brought some of the Jews he saved from the sack of Cartagena to the colonies.

For many years, the term was used as a racial slur in the South. It was applied mostly to multiracial families from the mid- to late nineteenth century. Following the passage of the Racial Integrity Act of 1924 in Virginia, many people buried their Melungeon ancestry for fear of being reclassified as black. By the twenty-first century, many Melungeons have been totally assimilated into American culture. Some of the most famous of these assimilated Melungeons are rumored to be Abraham Lincoln and Elvis Presley.

ROBERT JOHNSON, LEGENDARY BLUESMAN

Greenwood, Mississippi

On May 8, 1911, Robert Johnson was born in Hazlehurst, Mississippi, to a plantation worker named Noah Johnson and his wife, Julia. At a very early age, he realized that he did not want to spend the rest of his life sharecropping. He started playing the guitar in his teenage years by listening to blues greats on the radio like Charley Patton and Son House. In the 1930s, he struck out on his own as a blues singer. He sang in juke joints, levee camps and country suppers throughout the Arkansas and Mississippi Delta. Within a few months, Johnson and fellow bluesman Johnny Shines took their unique blend of blues to urban centers with large black populations, such as Chicago, Detroit and St. Louis. Johnson recorded his entire musical output in one session in November 1936 and in two sessions in June 1937. His promising career was cut short on the night of August 13, 1938, when he was poisoned by a jealous husband whose wife caught his eye while he was performing at a juke joint, the Three Forks, in Greenwood, Mississippi. Of the twenty-nine songs Johnson recorded, the most popular was "Terraplane Blues." Despite the brevity of his song catalogue, Robert Johnson is undoubtedly the most influential blues artist of all time, inspiring such artists as Eric Clapton, Bob Dylan, Keith Richards and Muddy Waters.

The rumors of Robert Johnson's Faustian bargain began after he left home and traveled to Arkansas. When he returned six months later, he could play guitar, some say, as well as any blues artist in Mississippi. Barry Lee

Pearson, coauthor of the book *Robert Johnson: Lost and Found*, believes that his contemporaries fabricated the story to make sense of his sudden burst of talent: "Everybody was so anxious to make this story true that they've been working on finding little details that can corroborate it," Pearson said. Son House contributed to the myth by stating that Robert Johnson was a good harmonica player but a poor guitarist until he vanished for a few weeks. The story goes that one day, Johnson met the devil at the crossroads of Highways 49 and 61. The devil took Johnson's guitar and returned it in exchange for his soul. When Johnson came home afterward, his guitar playing had improved considerably. Interestingly enough, this same story was told of bluesman Tommy Johnson years before. Belief in the origin of Johnson's talent has been bolstered by the titles of two of his songs: "Hell Hound on My Trail" and "Crossroads."

THE BOY PROPHET OF HAZLEHURST

Hazlehurst, Mississippi

At 6:00 a.m. on January 23, 1969, an F4 tornado hit the black community of Hazlehurst, Mississippi. The death toll—32—was high because many people were asleep. Injuries totaled 241. The tornado tracked through seven counties before finally weakening in Newton. That terrible day is still etched in many peoples' minds, not just because of the death and devastation, but also because of a strange little visitor who appeared in Hazlehurst three years before.

Longtime resident of Hazlehurst Steve Collins described the boy as being approximately ten years old with dark skin and curly black hair. His most distinctive physical characteristic was a dent at the top of the skull that enabled him to balance a pop bottle on his head as he walked around town talking about the Bible. Although some people mocked the boy and threw trash at him, others fed him and let him spend the night at their homes

Before long, people claimed that the boy had the power of prophecy. He told fortunes and, some say, healed people. One day, the local police charged him with vagrancy and tried to incarcerate him. He escaped from his handcuffs and leaped from the top of a tall wooden bridge. Eyewitnesses claim that his feet moved through the air as he fell, and he landed lightly on the ground without a scratch. The boy is remembered today for his prophetic announcement in the late 1960s that a terrible disaster would strike the town and change the residents' lives forever. People searched for the boy in the days following the tornado, but he was never found.

Steve Collins, who survived the tornado as a boy by hiding under the dead, plans on filming a documentary about the fateful day in the history of Hazlehurst. Collins never met the little boy, but he has interviewed over one hundred citizens of the town who have memories of meeting the strange little prophet. He hopes that the boy's true identity will come to light as a result of the publicity generated by his film.

8
NATIVE AMERICAN LEGENDS

LOVERS' LEAP OVERLOOK

Chattanooga, Tennessee

The Cherokee Indians originally settled in the Smoky Mountains around AD 1000. For the most part, they lived in villages of fifty log and mud huts. The Cherokees withdrew to the Blue Ridge Mountains in the late eighteenth century when large populations of European settlers moved into the area. Before long, the Cherokees began adopting the tools and weapons of the whites. Their lives changed forever in 1838 with the removal of the Cherokees from Tennessee. In the heart of downtown Chattanooga, a pedestrian walkway called Memorial Passage terminates at the steps of Ross Landing, which was one of three points of departure for the evacuation of the Cherokees by ships. Next to the stairway waterfall is a structure called "The Weeping Wall." It represents the tears shed by the Cherokees as they were forced to leave their nave lands.

Another tragic reminder of the Cherokee presence in the area is Lovers' Leap Overlook in Rock City Gardens, a popular tourist attraction approximately six miles outside of Chattanooga. Legend has it that an Indian brave named Sautee and a lovely Indian maiden named Nacoochee were lovers from warring tribes. Sautee was captured by a Cherokee raiding party and dragged to a ledge on top of Lookout Mountain. Grasping him

One of Rock City's attractions is Lovers' Leap, from which one can view seven states. *Flickr.*

by his arms and legs, several braves threw him off the mountain. While the Cherokees were watching Sautee plummet to his death on the rocks below, Nacoochee quietly walked over to the brink of the cliff. Before her family could stop her, she leaped from the overlook, screaming the name of her beloved: "Sautee."

THE SIREN OF THE FRENCH BROAD

Asheville, North Carolina

The French Broad River begins as a small stream in Rosman, North Carolina, and flows two hundred miles to Tennessee to form the Tennessee River. The name dates back to the 1700s when parts of western North Carolina were controlled by the French and the British. The broad rivers that cut through the region were referred to by the European settlers as "The French Broad River" and "The English Broad River." The Cherokee called the French Broad River a variety of names, including Agiqua (broad). The section of the river that runs down from Asheville was called Tahkeeosteh (racing waters).

The Cherokee believed that the Tahkeeosteh was the home of the Lorelei, sirens who appeared to male travelers who paused to refresh themselves by the pools where the water whirls and deepens. The story goes that when the man looks down into the water's surface, the face of a lovely woman appears, hypnotizing him with her gaze. At the same time, singing fills the air. Her face seems to be slightly out of focus, as if she is looking at him from a great distance. Suddenly, the traveler feels himself being pulled into the river by two cold, slimy arms. As the woman's face comes closer, it transforms itself into a grinning skull. As the man disappears under the water, spectral laughter echoes through the woods.

In a second version of the tale, the man sets up camp on the banks of the river. While the sun sinks below the horizon, the man crawls into his sleeping bag. Before long, he dreams of a beautiful, dark-haired woman. At the break of dawn, the traveler is awakened by the lilting tones of a woman's singing voice. He climbs out of the sleeping bag and makes breakfast. For the remainder of the day, he wanders along the bank of the river in a daze. That night, he returns to his tent and falls asleep. Once again, his dreams are haunted by the dark-haired woman. At midnight, he is awakened by the enchanting singing that had awakened him the night before. He becomes groggy as he stumbles to the riverside. He lies down and falls back to sleep. When he wakes up on the third day, the man resumes his walk along the river. When he reaches a certain bend of the river, he sits down and waits by the pool. At twilight, he stares transfixed into the dark water. Suddenly, a

Cherokee Indians living near what is now known as Asheville, North Carolina, told the story of beautiful dark-haired women who lured men to their deaths in the French Broad River. *Pollinator at en.wikipedia.*

voluptuous naked woman rises out of the water. She is singing to him. When he reaches out and touches her inviting arms, his fingers detect rough scales instead of soft, pliable flesh. Her claw-like hands grab his arms and drag him into the river. The traveler has become another hapless victim of the Siren of the French Broad.

THE LEGEND OF REELFOOT LAKE

Lake and Obion Counties, Tennessee

In the early nineteenth century, the rich bottomlands of the northeast corner of Tennessee were inhabited by a tribe of Chickasaw Indians. They lived in the shadow of the three-hundred-foot bluffs that lined the Mississippi River. At this time, the tribe was ruled by a chief whose son was born with a deformed foot. The deformity caused the young man to walk with a rolling motion, earning him the named Kalopin (Reelfoot). After his father died and Reelfoot became the chief, his thoughts turned to marriage. He decided to travel south to the lands of the Choctaws, whose women were rumored to be among the most beautiful in the land. He handpicked a group of warriors and set off down the river in a fleet of canoes.

After many days, the band of Indians arrived at the village of the great Choctaw chief Copiah. As Reelfoot approached the king's hut, he was stunned by the breathtaking beauty of the chief's daughter, sitting at his side. Reelfoot smoked the peace pipe and ate a meal of venison before revealing the true purpose of his visit. Reluctant to allow his daughter to marry a deformed brave, even a powerful one, Copiah listened to the young man's proposal and then informed him that his daughter could wed only a member of her own tribe.

Reelfoot was not deterred by the Chief's refusal. He offered to give Copiah an abundance of furs and pearls if he would give him his daughter's hand in marriage. Before making a decision, Copiah consulted a medicine man, who called out to the Great Spirit. After a while, the medicine man entered the king's hut and informed him that the chief's daughter must not be forcibly removed from her tribe by anyone. If Reelfoot stole her away from her own people, the earth would open up, and his entire village would be drowned. The fear of divine retribution moved Reelfoot to reconsider his marriage plans. He and his braves left the Choctaw village and turned

People say that Reelfoot Lake was inadvertently created by an Indian chief who angered the gods when he abducted a princess from a neighboring tribe. *JeremyA.*

their canoes north. That summer, Reelfoot could think of nothing else but Copiah's lovely daughter, Laughing Eyes. The forcefulness of the medicine man's words gradually faded with each passing day. When the autumn leaves began blowing in the wind, Reelfoot decided to return to the Choctaw village and steal the chief's daughter once the season had changed. He waited for the first snow to load the canoes with men and supplies and head south to the Choctaw village. Under the cover of darkness, Reelfoot and his men charged through the village and kidnapped the Choctaw princess. On the journey back to the Cherokee village, Laughing Eyes pleaded with Reelfoot to return her to her father before the Great Spirit's threat came to pass. However, now that Reelfoot had his heart's desire, not even the Great Spirit could make him change the course he had set upon.

On the night Reelfoot brought his bride home, the entire village rejoiced with dancing, singing and feasting. The celebration culminated in the marriage rites. Just before the ceremony was completed, the earth began to shake. The celebrants ran into the hills in a futile attempt to escape the wrath of the Great Spirit. Reelfoot and his bride realized too late that the Great Spirit had stamped his foot in anger. As the force of the New Madrid earthquake knocked the people to the ground, water engulfed the village and the entire valley, forming what is known today as Reelfoot Lake.

SPEARFINGER, THE CHEROKEE SHAPESHIFTER

Cleveland, Tennessee

Spearfinger is one of the most terrifying figures in Cherokee folklore. Cherokees living on the eastern side of Tennessee and the western part of North Carolina told the tale of a female ogre who was christened "Spearfinger" because the forefinger on her right hand resembled an obsidian knife. She was said to stab her victims in the heart or neck. She eviscerated her victims with her "spear finger" and consumed their livers. Her mouth was stained with the blood of the countless livers she had eaten. She had the ability to stab someone without being noticed. Sometimes, victims would not even realize that they had been stabbed until days later when they began "wasting away." She was also a shapeshifter who took the form of an old lady in order to approach children without scaring them away. Spearfinger frequently pounced on victims when they were picking strawberries or drinking from a stream.

In some villages, she was known as Nunyunui, which means "stone dress." This name refers to her stone-like skin. Because she was made of stone, Spearfinger "thundered" when she walked, crushing every rock in her path. Arrows bounced harmlessly off her thick hide. Her heart was in her right hand, which Spearfinger clutched tightly to protect it. Spearfinger's favorite hangout was Whiteside Mountain. Legend has it that she carried a great stone bridge to Whiteside Mountain, but higher beings struck it with lightning and destroyed it because it was too close to the upper World.

Spearfinger's only real enemy was a creature named Stone Man. They hated each other because they competed for the same food—livers. Unlike Spearfinger, who had to lift stones to erect huge structures, Stone Man was able to create bridges or towers simply by raising his staff.

Spearfinger was drawn to villages by their campfires. She also looked for plumes of smoke rising from the brush fires the Cherokees set on the mountainsides in their search for chestnuts. The possibility that an old lady seeking shelter for the night might be Spearfinger in disguise led the Cherokee to be fearful of strangers who entered their villages at night.

Eventually, the Cherokee devised a plan to rid themselves of Spearfinger forever. They dug a deep pit and covered it with brush. Then they produced a great cloud of smoke by setting fire to a pile of green saplings. Seeing the smoke, Spearfinger transformed herself into an old woman and ran to the village. Everyone was deceived except for the medicine man. He threw a spear at her, but it smashed into pieces on her stone skin. The other braves loosed their arrows at her, but they too were ineffectual. All at once, a chickadee flew out of the sky and landed on Spearfinger's right hand. The men immediately started shooting at her heart, concealed under her hand. One of the arrows hit the juncture of the wrist and the right hand, killing her instantly. The scourge of the Cherokee was dead at last.

9

LEGENDARY TREES

EMANCIPATION OAK

Hampton, Virginia

Standing at the entrance of Hampton University is the Emancipation Oak. The huge oak is ninety-eight feet tall and thirty inches in diameter. Because of the tree's history, the National Geographic Society has designated it as one of the Ten Great Trees of the World. The tree's historical significance dates to the Civil War. Between 1861 and 1865, the Union army under the command of General Benjamin F. Butler retained control of Fort Monroe, not far from the campus of Hampton University. At this time, the army used the fort as a sanctuary for escaped African American slaves, who were called "contraband" to prevent their former owners from demanding their return. In November 1861, a black teacher named Mary Smith Peake was asked by the American Missionary Association to teach the children in the contraband camp. Prior to 1861, she had been covertly teaching former slaves to read and write in direct violation of state law. Lacking a proper schoolhouse, she held her classes under an oak tree three miles away from Fort Monroe. Peake was a dedicated instructor who continued to teach, even when she was sick and bed-ridden. Eventually, adult freed men and freed women began attending class at night. Peake died in 1863. The massive oak tree received its name a few months later when African Americans heard a reading of Abraham Lincoln's Emancipation Proclamation under its branches.

In 1863, members of the Virginia Peninsula's African American community first learned of the signing of the Emancipation Proclamation under the sprawling branches of the southern live oak that has come to be known as the Emancipation Oak. *James Portell*.

Five years later, the biracial leadership of the AMA founded the Hampton Agricultural and Industrial School at the site of the Emancipation Oak. One of the school's first students was Booker T. Washington, who received his training as a teacher there. In 1878, Hampton opened its doors to Native Americans. In 1930, the school changed its name to Hampton Institute. In 1984, Hampton Institute acquired university status and changed its name to Hampton University.

Even though the Emancipation Oak has come to represent the university itself, its very existence was threatened in 2016 when the Virginia Department of Transportation (VDOT) announced plans to widen Interstate 64 leading into the Hampton Roads Bridge Tunnel. Not surprisingly, the university took legal action to oppose the destruction of its beloved oak tree. As of this writing, the Emancipation Oak still stands.

THE CART WAR OAK

Goliad, Texas

Goliad, Texas, is best known for what has come to be known as the "Goliad Massacre." On May 14, 1836, Colonel James W. Fannin was ordered by General Sam Houston to take his 400 men to Victoria because the Mexican army was closing in. Because Fannin moved his troops at a sluggish pace, Mexican general José de Urrea closed in on him at Coleta Creek. Realizing that his situation was hopeless, Fannin surrendered the next day. His forces were marched back to Goliad and imprisoned in the chapel at Fort Defiance. On March 27, 350 of Fannin's men were executed, almost twice the number of men who died at the Alamo. The ill will toward Mexicans was still running high in Goliad in the middle of the nineteenth century.

Between 1846 and 1870, court trials were held under the massive oak tree on the north side of the Goliad County Courthouse. The story goes that after the judge sentenced a convict to death, the execution was carried out immediately using one of the tree's many overhanging limbs as gallows. Goliad's most notorious hangings took place during the "Cart Wars." During the 1850s, Texas teamsters hauling freight between Indianola and San Antonio were losing business to Mexican teamsters who charged lower rates. In 1857, the resentment the Texas teamsters held for their Mexican counterparts reached its peak. In a series of bloody attacks, approximately seventy-five Mexican cart men were robbed and murdered. The Mexicans tried to bypass Goliad to avoid confrontations with the teamsters, but the attacks intensified.

Because local authorities chose to ignore that violence, a number of citizens registered complaints with the Mexican consulate. Concerned that the violence might erupt in an international incident, the governor of Texas petitioned the state legislature to provide funding for the use of the state militia as escorts for the Mexican cart men. Meanwhile, a group of local citizens decided to take the law into their own hands. The culprits were "tried" under the hanging oak and summarily lynched from its limbs. Bystanders say that several of the "cart-cutters" prayed just before execution, while others cursed the entire town. The old oak tree's bloody history has imbued it with an aura of mystery and infamy that attracts hundreds of visitors to the square every year. For locals, though, the Cart War Oak is a shady place to rest on hot summer days.

BOYINGTON OAK

Mobile, Alabama

Charles Boyington was an unemployed printer who arrived in Mobile from his home in Connecticut in 1830. For a short while, luck was with him. He was hired at the printing firm of Pollard and Dale soon after arriving. He also found lodgings in William George's boardinghouse. Boyington's roommate was a rather taciturn young man named Nathaniel Frost, but fellow boarders said that the two young men became close friends. When Frost was found bludgeoned to death just outside the Church Street Graveyard on May 11, 1834, Boyington's acquaintances told authorities of his fiery temper. When the police were told of Boyington's reputation as a gambler, the fact that Frost's pocket watch and sixty dollars in his pocket were stolen immediately came to mind.

Boyington received word that he was the primary suspect in the Frost murder case, so he quickly booked passage on a steamboat leaving Mobile, only to be arrested shortly thereafter. He was returned to Mobile on May 15. News accounts of Frost's murder portrayed Boyington as a fiend who killed his former friend "for the sake of plunder." Boyington was indicted for the murder of his friend. The judge scheduled his trial for November 21. After the prosecutor and the lawyer for the defense delivered their arguments, the jury deliberated for seventy-five minutes before delivering a verdict of guilty. Boyington was sentenced to hang on February 20, 1835. Just before the sentence was carried out, Boyington told the huge crowd of onlookers that a giant tree would grow from his grave as proof of his innocence. Boyington was buried in the northwest corner of the Church Street Graveyard. However, because the wall was moved back at the turn of the twentieth century, the grave is now located just outside the graveyard on the edge of Bayou Street, marked only by a massive oak tree. For many years, residents and visitors to Mobile have reported hearing weeping and whispering sounds coming from the grave site.

Just before he was hanged on February 20, 1835, Charles Boyington predicted that a giant oak tree would grow from his grave as proof of his innocence. The Boyington Oak now stands just outside the Church Street Graveyard on the edge of Bayou Street. *Wikimedia Commons*.

THE CRYING PECAN TREE OF CHOCTAW COUNTY

Needham, Alabama

On April 12, 1981, homeowner Linnie Jenkins was awakened by what she told a local newspaper editor seemed like the kind of whining sound a sleeping dog makes when it is dreaming. The next morning, Linnie and her son traced the source of the strange sound to the base of an immense seventy-five-foot-tall pecan tree in the front yard. After the *Choctaw Herald* published the story, people flocked to the sleepy little town of Needham from all over Alabama. Linnie recalled as many as four hundred people standing in her front yard at one time. A week after Linnie first heard the sound, the Jenkins family began charging visitors fifty cents a head to see the tree. CNN, which had just gotten started, sent a news crew to Needham. After the segment aired, people traveled to Choctaw County from all over the United States. A local storekeeper estimated that as many as three thousand people visited the Jenkinses' place on Easter Sunday. Some people compared the sounds to the whining of a puppy or the crying of a seal.

The sounds started becoming fainter in the first week of May, so the Jenkins family stuck a long metallic tube down a hole in the tree to make it easier to hear the sounds. After a while, the family sawed into the roots and dug in the ground to look for any signs of small animals. Linnie's son banged on the tree with a stick to see if the volume of the sound was affected. It was not.

Several theories were presented for the strange sounds once they ceased altogether. An entomologist suggested that the sounds were made by a rare beetle. A local forester blamed the sound on a gas-producing fungus. The strangest explanation came from neighbors who believed that the Jenkins house was built on top of an Indian burial mound. Indeed, members of the Jenkins family claimed that they could see strange figures walking around their house at night.

CAPTAIN TONY'S HANGING TREE

Key West, Florida

Captain Tony's Saloon at 428 Greene Street is reputed to be the oldest bar in Key West. Built in 1852, the building served as an icehouse first. Then it became Key West's first morgue. The ice, people said, kept their drinks and the bodies cool in hot weather. Over the years, the building was used as a cigar factory, a bootleg distillery, a bordello, a gambling house, a gay bar, a speakeasy and a telegraph station. News of the sinking of the USS *Maine* was first received here on February 15, 1898. Between 1933 and 1938, the building became a bar owned by Joe Russell. Its most famous patron was Ernest Hemingway, who visited the bar every day after spending the morning writing. When Russell moved the bar down the street, Hemingway laid claim to one of the urinals, which he used to "water" his cats. The next owner of the bar was a charter boat captain named Captain Tony Tarracino. He did his best to preserve the historical integrity of the building, including chains that secured the horses that pulled the ice wagons. Other historical artifacts include the tombstones of two women. Elvira Edmonds's tombstone was found under the floorboards in the 1980s, along with the remains of fifteen to eighteen people. Reba Sawyer's husband moved her tombstone to the bar, supposedly because she had a rendezvous with her lover there. Numerous bras hanging from the ceiling and hundreds of business cards on the walls stand as memorials to patrons from long ago.

Undoubtedly, the most fascinating of Captain Tony's "furnishings" is the so-called hanging tree, which the bar is built around. According to the legend, sixteen pirates, as well as a woman known only as "The Lady in Blue," were hanged from this tree in the early 1800s. Lady in Blue is said to have "chopped up" her husband and two sons with an axe. She then threw the bloody pieces of the corpses in the backyard for the birds and animals to "clean up." Exhausted from the work, she returned to the house and sat in a chair, her blue dress stained with the blood of her family. Some people say even her pale skin had turned a light shade of blue.

Unknown to the murderess, a nosy neighbor witnessed the woman's grisly disposal of the evidence of her crime. She immediately told her neighbors of the woman's heinous actions. The neighbors converged into an angry crowd that barged into the woman's house. When they viewed the murder scene, they immediately turned into a lynch mob. They grabbed the murderess and

Captain Tony's Saloon is known primarily as author Ernest Hemingway's "watering hole." However, it is also famous for the "hanging tree" that has grown through its roof. *Flickr*.

dragged her to the hanging tree, where she was strung up among the tree's spreading limbs.

The "Lady in Blue," as the woman has come to be known, has never left the site of her execution. Some patrons have caught a glimpse of a blue figure out of the corner of their eye. Others have seen what they described as a blue blur, streaking through the bar. The Lady in Blue's most terrifying manifestation took place in the ladies' restroom in January 2005. A female patron attempted to enter the first stall, but it was locked from the inside, so she entered the back stall instead. While she was there, she heard the outside door close. She peered through the door of her stall and was surprised to find that no one had entered the restroom. Suddenly, she heard the door of the first stall slam. She opened the door of the back stall and rushed over to the first stall. When she observed that the door to the first stall was still locked from the inside, she hurried out of the restroom. Other patrons informed her afterward that she had made the acquaintance of the Lady in Blue.

10

MYSTERIES FROM THE SKIES

THE KENTUCKY MEAT SHOWER

Bath, Kentucky

Charles Fort (1874–1932) was an American writer who specialized in strange phenomena. He devoted his entire life to collecting articles from newspapers, magazines and journals about scientific anomalies that were not covered well or were dismissed entirely by the scientific world, such as ball lightning, spontaneous human combustion, poltergeists, levitation and giant wheels of light. Some of the strangest occurrences covered in his seminal work *The Book of the Damned* (1919) are "falls" of frogs, fishes, black rain and inorganic matter, some of which happened centuries ago. One of the most famous of these falls took place in Bath, Kentucky, on March 3, 1876.

According to an article published in the *New York Times* on March 10, 1876, flakes of what appeared to be red meat fell from the sky for several minutes near the house of Allen Crouch. His wife, who was making soap outside at the time, said that the flakes resembled "large snowflakes." The flakes ranged in size from one to four inches in diameter. In *The Book of the Damned*, Charles Fort wrote that the flakes fell "in a thick shower, on the ground, on trees, on faces, but it was narrowly localized upon a strip of land about 100 yards long and 50 yards wide." Two men who were bold enough to eat small portions of the meat responded that it tasted like rancid venison or mutton. A local hunter who examined the material identified it as "bear meat." However, not everyone agreed.

The Kentucky Meat Shower received a great deal of media coverage, including articles that appeared in scientific journals. In an article published in the *Medical Record*, Dr. Allan McLane Hamilton stated that the meat samples were lung tissue from human infants or horses. In *The Sanitarian*, Leopold Brandeis went on record as stating that the flakes were not meat at all: "The Kentucky 'wonder' is no more or less than nostoc," which he described as a type of bacteria that forms colonies enveloped in a gelatinous covering. Dr. J.W.S. Arnold concluded in the *American Journal of Microscopy and Popular Science* that the meat flakes were actually lung tissue and animal cartilage.

Although the type of meat that fell from the sky on March 3, 1876, was never officially determined by scientists, locals were fairly certain that the meat had been disgorged by buzzards flying over Bath, Kentucky. Several outdoorsmen observed that when one buzzard vomits, others follow suit. Even a scientist, Dr. L.D. Kastenbine, accepted the "buzzard vomit" theory in an article published in the 1876 edition of the *Louisville Medical News*. He noted that some vultures vomit as a defense mechanism while trying to escape an enemy. No one has speculated as to how many buzzards would have been required to projectile vomit that much meat.

THE AURORA INCIDENT

Aurora, Texas

Over fifty years before the Roswell incident popularized the term "UFO" (unidentified flying object), the imagination of Americans was captivated by phenomena newspapers referred to as "mystery airships." The best known of these sightings occurred between 1896 and 1897. Sightings of cigar-shaped airships were reported from the entire country. This wave of airship reports began with a sighting in California in 1896. Some of these reports included encounters with passengers aboard the ships and even with the pilots. Approximately 1,500 newspapers covered these sightings, the most famous of which happened in Aurora, Texas.

S.E. Hayden ignited a firestorm of publicity for his hometown when he wrote his account of a mystery airship in the April 17, 1897 edition of the *Dallas Morning News*. In his story, Hayden reported that at 6:00 a.m., an airship traveling between ten and twelve miles an hour soared over the public square, headed toward the north part of town. It crashed into Judge J.S. Proctor's windmill and exploded, scattering debris over several acres and destroying the judge's flower garden. The spacecraft was too damaged for investigators to determine the means of propulsion. Metallic fragments found on the scene appeared to be a mixture of aluminum and silver. Hayden wrote that residents found an extraterrestrial in the wreckage: "The pilot of the ship is supposed to have been the only one on board, and while his remains are disfigured, enough of the original has been picked up to show that he was not an inhabitant of this world." Hayden ends the article with an announcement of the alien's burial, which was to be held at noon the next day at the local cemetery. Locals now refer to the alien as "Ned."

Supposedly, residents dumped the wreckage in a well conveniently located under the windmill. Some believe that part of the wreckage was placed in the grave with the corpse of the pilot. In 1935, the crash site was purchased by Brawley Oates, who removed the wreckage from the well. However, after contracting arthritis, Oates set a concrete slab over the well and constructed an outbuilding on top of the slab.

In the twenty-first century, the Aurora Cemetery has become the focus of attention for many UFO enthusiasts. In 2005, the Mutual UFO Network (MUFON) visited the cemetery. The members found a grave marker depicting a flying saucer but were denied permission to exhume the body of the alien. In 2008, the grandson of Brawley Oates gave investigators associated with the television show *UFO Hunters* permission to unseal the well. The team found unusually high traces of aluminum in the water, but nothing else. The investigators also examined an unmarked grave in the 1890s section of the Aurora Cemetery using ground-penetrating radar but were unable to determine what types of bones were present.

Not surprisingly, the alien's grave site has fascinated UFO aficionados and curiosity seekers for generations, especially the grave marker. It was stolen in 1972, and a replacement marker was stolen in 2012. Visitors have added their own inscriptions, such as "Rest in peace, my alien brother."

THE KELLY-HOPKINSVILLE GREEN MAN CASE

Kelly-Hopkinsville, Kentucky

On August 21, 1955, Billy Ray Taylor and his wife were spending the night in the Sutton family's farmhouse in Kelly, Kentucky. Billy was drawing water from the well when he caught sight of a large, shining object landing a quarter of a mile away. No one believed him when he returned to the house with the bucket of water, but their disbelief vanished a short time later when the family dogs started barking. Elmer "Lucky" Sutton and Billy Ray picked up their guns and went out the door. They had not walked very far before they saw a strange little creature coming toward them. It stood between three and four feet tall and held its hands in the air. When it got closer, the two men could tell that it had large eyes, a thin mouth, large ears and short legs. At the end of its arms were claw-like hands. Terrified, the men fired their weapons repeatedly, but the strange little being seemed to be unharmed as it ran into the woods.

The men turned around and ran back toward the house. As soon as they were inside, they noticed another creature's face looking at them through the window. They fired their guns once again, blasting a large hole through the window screen. The men ran back out the door, but the creature was nowhere to be found. They ran back inside the house and shut the door. Soon, Billy Ray, Lucky and the other nine members of their family found themselves being attacked by a band of twelve to fifteen of these extraterrestrial visitors. They fired through the windows at the creatures, going through four boxes of .22 pistol shells. One of the "things" perched on top of the roof and grabbed at the hands of one of the people inside.

The alien invaders continued tormenting the inhabitants of the farmhouse well into the night. Realizing that they needed outside help to fight the menacing creatures, Billy Ray and Lucky loaded their families into two cars and drove to the police station in Hopkinsville. The family's insistence that their fantastic tale really happened eventually convinced the skeptical sheriff that there might be truth to their claims, and he agreed to follow them to the Sutton farmhouse. Twenty officers searched the property for evidence of the strange invaders but found nothing more than bullet holes in the walls and windows. They left the farmhouse convinced that the eleven occupants had been genuinely frightened by something that night. Not long after the police left, the aliens resumed their attack on the farmhouse.

The next morning, the police department persuaded the U.S. Air Force to investigate the incident. Four military policemen interviewed the family members about the strange events of the night before. They also walked around the perimeter of the house but found nothing out of the ordinary. Rumors of the strange encounter at the Sutton farm soon spread throughout the county. The story was published in the *Kentucky New Era*, the local newspaper, on August 22, 1955. The sketches made from the witnesses' individual descriptions of the aliens bore an uncanny resemblance. A year later, noted ufologist Dr. J. Allen Hynek conducted his own investigation of the assault on the Sutton farmhouse and concluded that the incident was genuine. Eventually, accusations from their neighbors that the Suttons had perpetrated a hoax proved to be too much. Ten days later, the family left town for good.

Today, the aliens' arrival is commemorated in Kelly, Kentucky's annual Little Green Men Days Festival. Since 2005, as many as twenty thousand visitors have traveled to the two-day festival, which features an outdoor film viewing, vendors, writers and an alien costume contest. The Little Green Men Festival is truly an out-of-this-world event.

THE BETZ MYSTERY SPHERE

Fort George Island, Florida

One of the nation's strangest extraterrestrial visitations took place on Fort George Island on May 26, 1974. Gerri and Antoine Betz, along with their son, twenty-one-year-old Terri Matthew Betz, were inspecting the damage done to their eighty-eight-acre plot of woodland by a brush fire when they made an astounding discovery in the charred brush: a gigantic metal sphere. The polished orb was eight inches in diameter and weighed twenty-two pounds. On close examination, the family noticed an elongated triangle engraved on the surface of the sphere. At first, they assumed that the strange-looking object was an old cannonball someone had silver-plated as a souvenir. The family members loaded up the sphere in their car and brought it home. Terry set it on a window seat in his bedroom and did not pay much attention to it for two weeks. Then one day, while he was playing guitar for a friend, the sphere began vibrating and making a throbbing sound. The family dog whined and cowered in the presence of the sphere. Over the next few days, the sphere began acting even more strangely. When someone pushed the ball away, it always returned to its original position. When hit by a hammer, the sphere emitted a ringing sound. Supposedly, the globe also caused doors to open and close and produced organ music that played throughout the house. After observing the sphere for a while, the family theorized that NASA must have dropped it from the sky onto their property.

Before long, the sphere began attracting the attention of the scientific world. Ufologist and astronomer J. Allen Hynek arranged for five scientists in New Orleans to examine the sphere. They determined that it was manmade, not extraterrestrial. The U.S. Navy studied the globe at the Jacksonville Naval Air Station and found that its half-inch-thick shell was made of stainless steel and an unknown element. Dr. James Albert Harder, an engineering professor emeritus at the University of California–Berkeley, studied the globe in 1977 and concluded that it had atomic numbers higher than 140 and was potentially explosive. Soon after Dr. Herder delivered his findings, the sphere vanished without a trace. So far, the origin of the Betz Mystery Sphere has not been conclusively determined.

THE WYTHEVILLE UFO SIGHTINGS

Wytheville, Virginia

In October 1987, radio station WYVE was barraged with telephone calls from residents of Wytheville, Virginia, claiming to have seen UFOs in the night sky. The news director, Dan Gordon, remained skeptical, assuming that what people were seeing was military aircraft. Gordon's cynicism vanished on the night of October 21 when he and a friend, Roger Hall, drove to a place near Wytheville where most of the sightings took place. In an interview Gordon gave on November 4, 1987, he said that he and his friend had been driving four and a half miles on Route 21 south of Wytheville when he looked to his left and saw something strange in the sky:

> *I stopped the car and got out. As it approached, it looked like it had…the front shape was kinda like a funny-looking, round front to a craft, with a long, split cockpit….It had a strobe that was putting out five different colors of lights on the right side of the craft. I told my friend to get out….We were pretty astounded just from what we saw coming toward us.*

The men were so transfixed by the strange object that they forgot that there were two cameras in the trunk of the car. Gordon's friend, who was a former pilot, estimated that the spacecraft was between eight and nine hundred feet long. The men also noticed that the object made no sound at all as it slowly moved approximately two thousand feet above ground level. On the rear of the spacecraft were what appeared to be three windows.

The men stared at the object until it disappeared behind a cloud. Suddenly, a large red sphere appeared on the left. It flew parallel to the ground at a high rate of speed until it vanished from sight. The men then confirmed that they had both seen the same thing.

Gordon returned the next night with his friend Roger Hall, Hall's friend John Stember and Stember's girlfriend. Two miles up the road, they found the same spacecraft hovering over the dirt road to the left. "We started shooting with videotape and the two film cameras," Gordon said.

Afterward, the men decided to go public with their findings. A press conference was scheduled for the next day, October 23. The night before the conference, Gordon received an anonymous phone call from someone who said that the CIA was very interested in his encounter. Over the next hours, Gordon received several other calls warning him not to interfere with the government's business. Despite the warnings, Gordon went ahead with the press conference. When he returned home, he was shocked to find that someone had broken into his house; oddly enough, nothing was taken.

Six weeks later, Gordon, his wife and their daughter were walking to their car from the local mall when a crowd of people began screaming and pointing to the sky. Gordon looked up and saw a large flying object that broke into four fragments. As Gordon began photographing them, the UFOs transformed themselves from teardrop-shaped objects to ball-shaped objects to disc-shaped objects. Before flying off, the UFOs changed once again, this time into egg shapes.

By the end of December, over 1,500 sightings of UFOs had been reported in Wytheville. A representative of the Department of Defense told Gordon the UFOs the people of Wytheville had seen were real but that they posed no real threat to anyone. On March 19, 1988, while packing for a broadcasters' conference in Virginia Beach, Gordon received a telephone call from a man who claimed to be a retired military officer. He began the conversation by advising Gordon to record the phone call. The official informed Gordon that his son had died of leukemia because of his UFO research, and he was concerned that the same thing might happen to Gordon.

Gordon continued receiving strange phone calls over the next few weeks. One day, he was visited by two men who identified themselves as newspaper reporters. One of them interviewed Gordon for forty-five minutes while the other reporter took photographs throughout the house. Afterward, Gordon called the local newspaper and found that no men matching this description worked there.

A couple of months later, Gordon set about organizing his UFO photographs. He had not been working very long before realizing that the negatives for the mall parking lot images were missing. He looked at the photographs to see if there was something in them that he had not caught the first time he had examined them. When Gordon could not find a reason why someone would want to steal the negatives, he asked other people to examine the photographs as well, but they could not find anything either.

The stress of dealing with the mysteries connected with the Wytheville sightings contributed to his physical and emotional collapse two months later. While recovering at home, Gordon remembered the retired military man's warning that UFO research could be bad for his health. After Wytheville sighting mania died out in December 1990, Gordon dispensed with hunting for flying saucers.

THE PASCAGOULA ALIEN ABDUCTION

Pascagoula, Mississippi

On October 11, 1973, forty-two-year-old Charles Hickson and nineteen-year-old Calvin Parker had just gotten off work at the shipyard. They decided to do a little fishing off a pier in front of an old abandoned shipyard in Pascagoula. At 6:00 p.m., Parker observed a blue light reflecting off the water. Parker said that in the darkness, the flashing blue light resembled "a bright moon." With a great deal of difficulty, Parker was able to make out in the "blinding light" an object shaped like a football eighty feet wide and ten feet high. It levitated two feet above the ground. Parker recalled that the huge craft made surprisingly little noise, just a hissing sound.

Parker said he and Hickson were conscious but paralyzed while three gray humanoid creatures levitated them aboard the ship. The aliens had no necks and were about five feet tall. They seemed to glide over the ground with their jointed pedestal-like legs. Their ears and noses were nothing more than carrot-shaped protrusions. Under hypnosis, Parker recalled being examined by an oval-shaped mechanical eye for fifteen to twenty minutes. Afterward, Parker and Hickson were returned to the pier. Stunned, they sat in their car for forty-five minutes before reporting the incident to the sheriff. They both passed polygraph tests in the police station.

Within a few days, the story of the pair's abduction by aliens had spread throughout Pascagoula. Reporters from across the country descended on the town. Parker and Hickson were interviewed by the director of Project Blue Book, J. Allen Hynek, and by a representative of the Aerial Phenomena Research Organization, James Harder. Hynek concluded that the fisherman "had a very real, frightening experience." Harder, on the other hand, believed that Parker and Hickson had actually experienced extraterrestrial phenomena. Hickson made the best of the unwanted publicity he received, giving interviews and writing a book, *UFO Contact at Pascagoula* (1983). Parker, however, tried to distance himself from his traumatic experience. He finally came to terms with it in 2018 with the publication of his book *Pascagoula—The Closest Encounter: My Story*.

THE CASH-LANDRUM INCIDENT

Huffman, Texas

At 9:00 p.m. on December 29, 1980, Betty Cash and Vickie Landrum, along with Vickie's seven-year-old grandson, Colby Landrum, were driving back home to Dayton, Texas, on a two-lane road in a heavily wooded area near Huffman, Texas. While navigating the heavily wooded area, they observed a light in the sky. The women assumed that it was just an airplane until it came close. They described it later as a diamond-shaped object that emitted heat and flames. Cash tried to turn the car around, but the road was too narrow and the shoulder was soft and muddy. The women stopped the car and approached the object. They described the floating object as resembling the Dayton water tower with its top and bottom removed. The center was ringed with small blue lights. When the engine flamed, the object moved farther down the road. Heat from the object made their car painful to touch. The vinyl dashboard had been so softened by the heat that one of the women's hands made a deep imprint in its surface. Suddenly, without warning, the object rose into the sky. After it had cleared the treetops, a group of twenty-three helicopters surrounded it. The helicopters and the object receded into the distance. The entire incident lasted only twenty minutes. Detective Lamar Walker and his wife told investigators that they saw twelve Chinook-type helicopters in the area where Cash and Landrum had had their experience, but they did not see a large diamond-shaped object.

That night, Cash, Vickie and Colby suffered from nausea, diarrhea and vomiting. In addition, they experienced a burning sensation in their eyes and skin. A few days later, Cash had blisters on her skin and had difficulty walking. When she was admitted to the hospital on January 3, 1981, large patches of skin had peeled off and clumps of hair had fallen out. Vickie and Colby also suffered hair loss and skin eruptions, but to a lesser extent. A radiologist determined that they had been exposed to ionizing radiation with a possible infrared or ultraviolet component as well.

The only formal investigation of the incident was conducted in 1982 by Lieutenant Colonel George Sarran of the Department of the Army Inspector General. He admitted that the women were credible witnesses, but he was unable to trace the helicopters to the U.S. Army. Undeterred, Cash and Landrum sought monetary compensation for their injuries. With the help of their lawyer, Peter Gersten, they sued the U.S. government for $20 million. On August 21, 1986, their case was dismissed by a U.S. District Court judge because the plaintiffs had not proven that the helicopters were connected with the U.S. government.

11

UNDERWATER MYSTERIES

THE UNDERWATER GRAVEYARD

Manasota Key, Florida

In 2016, an amateur diver swimming near Manasota Key was searching for the fossilized teeth of a megalodon when he made a totally unexpected find. While sifting through the peat on the ocean bottom, he discovered a human jaw bone with a single molar. He brought the bone home and placed it on a paper plate. Two weeks later, he sent a photograph of what he thought might be human remains to Florida's Bureau of Archaeological Research. The bureau's supervisor, Ryan Duggins, suspected that the jaw bone was probably prehistoric because the tooth was worn smooth from eating tough food. Duggins and his researchers found the spot three hundred feet off shore in twenty-one feet of water. When the team found three human skulls and several wooden stakes, Duggins realized that the shark tooth diver had stumbled upon an ancient burial site that had been preserved in a peat bog.

His team returned to the site in 2017 to retrieve a small test unit. Using pastry brushes and chopsticks, the researchers were able to penetrate the layers of sea bottom and peat. This time, they found textile fragments in addition to more wooden stakes and bones. Radiocarbon tests of the wooden stakes revealed that the graveyard was around seven thousand years old. Duggins believes that the site was originally a shallow peat-bottomed pond back when the area was ten feet above sea level. Duggins deduced from the evidence that the native inhabitants of the area wrapped the corpses in handwoven cloth and sank them to the bottom of the pond. Several fire-hardened stakes were probably pounded into the pond bed around the bodies with tops protruding above the water line to mark the location of the graves.

At the time of this printing, Duggins's team had found the bones of six individuals. However, he believes that the archaeologists will find many more remains. In fact, the complete graveyard may cover more than an acre.

THE OUTER BANKS' MYSTERY ISLAND

Cape Hatteras, North Carolina

In the fall of 2016, residents of the Outer Banks were startled by the sudden emergence of a hook-shaped island from the ocean depths near Cape Hatteras. At first, many people assumed that the strange land mass was nothing more than a sand bar that would be short-lived. They were surprised when the island continued growing throughout 2017, reaching a size of twenty-seven acres. NASA scientists asserted that ideal weather conditions were probably responsible for the island's development:

> *Winds were strong enough to stir up the waves and currents that carry sand alongshore from the more northerly barrier islands toward the cape. Then winds became calm enough for* [the] *transport to be halted by obstacles such as circular currents within Hatteras Light and the expansive shoals of the cape. Sand accumulated, an island grew, and tourists flocked to the area to witness the spectacle.*

Investigators from the U.S. Navy soon discovered that the brand-new island contained a plethora of curiosities. These included barnacle-encrusted nautical instruments from the nineteenth and twentieth centuries, as well as model bombs and live bombs. Because of the large number of sea shells on the island, it was christened "Shelly Island." It soon became a popular destination for tourists attracted to the unique qualities of its shells.

By the end of 2017, photographs taken by NASA's Landsat 8 satellite indicated that the island was receding into the ocean. NASA credited erosion brought on by Hurricanes Irma, Jose and Maria in September for the island's disappearance. The storms cut the island in half. The portion that was unconnected to the mainland was eventually washed away by winter storms.

ALABAMA'S UNDERWATER FOREST

Mobile, Alabama

In 2004, Hurricane Ivan roared through the Gulf of Mexico as a Category 5 with ninety-eight-foot-tall waves. Before Ivan made landfall, its winds scooped out about ten feet of sediment and uncovered an ancient bald cypress forest. One of the fishermen who found the site, Chas Broughton, notified scientists about the unusual discovery. The first scientific investigation of the ancient trees took place in 2012. The scientists discovered that the site covered approximately two city blocks under sixty feet of seawater in Mobile Bay. They theorized that when sea levels rose sixty thousand years ago during an ice age, the trees were buried under mud and sediment with low oxygen levels. As a result, the bacteria that cause wood to rot were unable to thrive inside the trees.

Now that the forest has been exposed to the elements, the wood is beginning to decompose. Scientists are eager to study the trees before they are gone forever. Kristine De Long, a paleoclimatologist at Louisiana State University, believes that the forest could reveal how climate change affects the future. "These trees died very quickly, and we want to see how that's tied to sea level rise," DeLory said. Ben Raines, who organized the first scientific exploration of the site, was amazed when he saw the trees for the first time: "You're in this sort of ethereal fairy world, where the stumps are covered in anemones and everything," he said. "But you realize they are trees."

12

LEGENDARY LOCATIONS

THE BIZARRE HISTORY OF THE CRESCENT HOTEL

Eureka Springs, Arkansas

In 1884, the Eureka Improvement Commission hired Missouri architect Isaac Taylor to design a luxury hotel on twenty-seven acres. The developers chose this site, known locally as Glenwood Park, because of the nearby springs, which were reputed to have healing powers. Taylor's designs drew from several architectural styles. The building's most distinctive features are its eighteen-inch-thick granite walls and numerous towers. Landscapers decorated the lawn with beautiful gardens, boardwalks and gazebos. Croquet and tennis courts were built for the guests' outdoor enjoyment. Construction of the resort spa was completed at a cost of $294,000. The hotel opened its doors for business on May 1, 1880. The guest speaker at the open house ceremony was James B. Blaine, the Republican presidential nominee. In 1901, the annex addition was built. The twelve new rooms accommodated the growing need for more housing. That same year, C.H. Smith from St. Louis purchased the hotel from the Eureka Improvement Company for $30,000. The following year, the Frisco Railroad leased the Crescent Hotel.

From 1902 to 1907, the Crescent Hotel flourished. Well-to-do guests from across the nation flocked to the hotel to take advantage of the spring's

Built in 1886 as a resort for the rich and famous, the Crescent Hotel has also served as a Conservatory for Women and, most notoriously, as a cancer clinic. *Alan Brown*.

curative powers and the Crescent's amenities, which included a bowling alley, afternoon tea parties, billiards tables and modern plumbing. By 1907, however, profits plummeted as the hotel's clientele began questioning the healing powers of the spring water.

After the Fresco Railroad declined to renew its lease, the Crescent College and Conservatory for Women took over the former hotel. During this period in the building's history, it served as a hotel only during the summer months of 1908–23 and 1929–33. The boarding school, which was opened by the Eureka Springs Investment Company, was a nondenominational Christian girls' school. Tuition was expensive: $270 a year in 1909–10 and $375 in 1912. Between eighty and one hundred students boarded there each year. The same number of local (day) students attended the conservatory. The school uniform consisted of a white dress in the fall and spring and a dark blue suit with blouse for the winter. The curriculum consisted of classes in art, music, literature, domestic science and a number of commercial courses. The costs of maintaining the large building were so steep that not even the sky-high tuition was enough to run the school.

The school closed its doors in 1924. It opened briefly from 1930 to 1934 as a junior college. Then in 1937, a self-proclaimed physician named Norman Baker bought the building with the intention of converting it into a "health resort" for cancer patients. In actuality, "Dr." Baker was a charlatan from Muscarine, Iowa. He set up his cancer clinic at Eureka Springs after the authorities closed his Muscarine hospital—the Baker Institute—because he was practicing medicine without a license. He transferred 144 of his patients from Muscarine to the Baker Hotel, where he treated them with his "miraculous cure," consisting of alcohol, carbolic acid and glycerin. As soon as the doors of his new cancer clinic opened, Baker set about adding his own personal touches to the former luxury hotel. He painted entire sections of the hotel purple, even the Venetian blinds. Baker replaced the beautiful wooden balconies and railings with concrete. In his office, the former Governor's Suite, Baker hung two submachine guns on the wall. A secret staircase in Baker's office led up to his girlfriend's room. Baker's fashion accessories included white shirts and lavender ties. He even drove a lavender automobile. In 1947, Baker's reign ended when he was sentenced to Leavenworth Penitentiary for four years for using the mails to defraud.

As is the case with many mysterious enterprises, legends have been generated to fill in the gaps in the historical record. It is said that workers remodeling the hotel discovered human skeletons concealed inside the walls. Jars of preserved body parts are said to be hidden throughout the hotel. People familiar with Baker's surgical technique claimed that he opened his patients' skulls and poured his tonic directly on their brains. Legend has it that the corpses of patients who had died under his care were hidden for weeks before being burned in the incinerator. Advanced cancer cases were placed in a special asylum, where they eventually passed away after considerable suffering.

The former Crescent Hotel stood empty until 1946, when four Chicago businessmen bought the building from Baker's girlfriend, Thelma Young, to whom he had left the bulk of his property. The sale price was $45,000. Dwight Nichols, the resident manager for twenty-five years, set aside $20,000 for renovations. Baker's Dutch doors were replaced, and the garish red, orange, black and yellow paint that he had used to cover up the woodwork was removed. Even his scaled-down replica of the Statue of Liberty, which commemorated the year the famous statue and the Crescent Hotel were erected, was pulled down. The investors brought the crowds back to the hotel by offering package vacations. Approximately 90 percent of the guests were women. Over the next twenty-five years, air conditioners were

The corpses of Dr. Norman Baker's patients were transported down to the morgue, where they were stored in the walk-in freezer, examined and disposed of in the incinerator. *Alan Brown.*

installed in the windows, a dance platform was built in the parking lot and new furnishings for fifty rooms were purchased. Nichols himself broadcast a radio show from the lobby bar. In 1967, the hotel was closed down as the result of a fire in the elevator shaft.

In 1973, the Crescent Heights Development Company purchased the Crescent Hotel for $198,000 for the purpose of demolishing it and selling the limestone. However, Lowana Feagins persuaded the new owners to restore the old hotel instead. Belgian chandeliers and new ceilings and carpeting were installed, and new draperies and tablecloths were added to the dining room. In addition, the bathrooms were renovated, and a new boiler replaced the old one.

In 1980, Bob Feagins and his second wife, Glenda, sold the Crescent Hotel to the National Historic Registry Hotels of Eureka Springs. Improvements included the installation of a new swimming pool, new coats of paint on the walls and the creation of a new lobby bar. Because of the mounting costs of renovations and the reductions allowed for tax credits, the owners of the Crescent Hotel filed for bankruptcy in 1988.

In 1993, Gary and Carole Clawson from Florence, Oregon, bought the hotel and hired a manager to run it. The Clawsons built fire escapes for the penthouse and rebuilt the ice cream parlor. The couple emphasized cleanliness and good food.

Marty and Elise Roenigk, who had previously owned antique shops, bought the Basin Park Hotel and the Crescent Hotel in 1997. They replaced the entire roof on the annex and structural beams. In addition, they repaired the parking lot, created four Jacuzzi suites, redesigned the gardens and added a beauty salon and bridal room to transform the historic hotel into a venue for weddings. Their pet project, the New Moon Spa and Salon, is the second-largest spa in the Ozarks. The spa includes Vichy showers, a hydrotherapy tub, a sauna, tanning beds and exercise equipment. The improvements amounted to well over $1 million.

Not surprisingly, the horrific history of the Crescent Hotel has generated a large number of ghost stories. The lobby is haunted by the ghost of Dr. Baker. He has been sighted wearing a white linen suit and a purple shirt. Witnesses have identified the ghost from actual photographs of Dr. Baker.

The presence of Dr. Norman Baker has been sensed around his desk, which now sits in the lobby of the Crescent Hotel. *Alan Brown.*

One wonders if Dr. Baker's spirit is attached to his desk, which sits in the book/T-shirt area of the lobby.

The Crystal Dining Room is also said to be haunted. One of the ghosts is the figure of a man dressed in Victorian-era clothes. This outgoing spirit has been known to engage in conversations with guests. Some witnesses claim that the ghost informed them that he is looking for a young woman he met at a party in the dining room the night before. A cook at the Crescent Hotel had a couple of unnerving experiences in the dining room. One morning, while he was slicing carrots, he looked up and saw a little boy wearing "pop bottle" glasses and old-fashioned pants skipping around the kitchen for a few seconds before he disappeared. Not long thereafter, the cook entered the kitchen and turned on the lights, just as he had done hundreds of mornings before. Without warning, several pots and pans flew off their hooks. This was definitely not the way he had planned to start his day.

Another Victorian-era ghost haunting the hotel is the spirit of Dr. John Freemont Ellis, the physician for the Crescent Hotel. His office was in what is now room 212. He has been sighted wearing a top hat and walking down the main staircase. Some eyewitnesses describe him as being dressed for one of the balls held in the hotel in the 1880s.

A rather taciturn figure known only as the "quiet ghost" has manifested around the hotel lobby, possibly because it has been decorated in the Victorian style. He is a distinguished-looking gentleman with a moustache and a beard. His attire dates to the Victorian era. The ghost is usually seen sitting in a chair. People who walk up to him and try to engage him in conversation report that he never responds to their questions. After a few seconds, he fades away.

The most requested room in the hotel is room 218. In 1885, one of the Irish stonemasons hired to build the hotel fell to his death just about where the room is now located. Michael, as he has come to be known, announces his presence in a variety of ways. The door to the room occasionally opens and shuts on its own. Guests in room 218 have encountered strange sounds and uncomfortable sensations. A salesman who was sleeping in the room claimed that something shook him by the shoulders and woke him up. As he adjusted his eyes to the dark, the man heard the distinct sound of footsteps. Afterward, the salesman said that it sounded as if someone was walking very briskly across the room. Another guest was so terrified by the sight of ghostly blood splatter on the walls that he ran screaming out of the room.

Not surprisingly, room 218 is popular with paranormal investigators. The second most-requested room is 419, otherwise known as "Theodora's

Right: Use of this antique switchboard was discontinued after it began receiving telephone calls from the now empty basement. *Alan Brown*.

Below: The Crystal Dining Room is haunted by the figure of a gentleman dressed in Victorian-era clothing who asks guests if they have seen a woman he met the night before. *Alan Brown*.

Room." She is believed to have been one of Dr. Baker's cancer patients in the late 1930s. Theodora is said to be a very fastidious spirit who reorganizes the room if she perceives that the guests have been messy. She has even been known, on occasion, to throw clothes out of the door if they had been lying on the floor of the bedroom. Some guests believe that she is the one who turns the key in the lock. Supposedly, she has even introduced herself as a cancer patient to people staying in the room.

The most haunted floor in the hotel is the third floor. The apparition of a nurse has been sighted pushing a gurney down the hallway late at night. The most haunted room on the floor—3500—is one of the rooms in the annex. A female spirit clothed in a Victorian-style nightgown is said to haunt room 3500. She is believed to have been one of Dr. Baker's cancer patients housed in the former servants' quarters when they were in the final stages of the disease. The screams of "asylum patients," as they were called, could not be heard because the annex was cut off from the rest of the building.

My wife, Marilyn, and I had our own encounter with the ghost in room 3500 when we stayed at the hotel July 6–7, 2018. On the night of July 7, I began my investigation by taking readings with my EMF detector and thermal thermometer. I then asked the spirit to answer my questions by turning a flashlight on and off, but I received no reply. Meanwhile, Marilyn captured several orbs in the room on her camera. The next morning, I packed the suitcases and carried them out to the car. When I returned to the room, Marilyn was sitting in a chair next to the coffee table with a stricken look on her face. She told me that shortly after I left the room, she was sitting in the chair, looking at her phone, when suddenly, my Yeti glass flew off the table. It landed a couple of feet from the coffee table. Marilyn believes that the female ghost made its presence known to her because both of them had had cancer. Before we checked out, Marilyn told one of the clerks in the lobby about her unnerving experiences in room 3500. Because so many guests have had similar stories, she was not surprised by our experience. She was disappointed, though, because we did not video the ghostly activity.

Not surprisingly, the Crescent Hotel is generally regarded as one of the most haunted hotels in the United States. Although the hotel's ghost stories had been documented for years in books like Frances Kermeen's *Ghostly Encounters: True Stories of America's Haunted Inns and Hotels* (2002) and Michael Norman and Beth Scott's *Haunted America* (1994), the hotel did not acquire its national reputation as a haunted hotel until Jason Hawes and his team of investigators filmed an episode of *Ghost Hunters* there in 2005. The team's most astounding piece of evidence was the image of a human being captured on the thermal camera. After this episode aired, the number of visitors to the Crescent Hotel increased dramatically. Instead of downplaying its ghostly occurrences, as some hotels do, the Crescent celebrates them. Not only does it have its own line of ghost-related merchandise, but it also gives nightly ghost tours inside the hotel. Granted, not everyone stays at the Crescent Hotel in the hope of collecting evidence of the paranormal, but many of the people who do spend the night for that very reason are not disappointed.

On February 5, 2019, evidence supporting many of the stories concerning Norman Baker's nefarious activities was uncovered by the hotel's landscape gardener, Susan Benson. While she and a work crew were expanding a parking pad at the north end of the property, they uncovered several medicine bottles, some of which contained objects floating in a clear liquid. The expansion project was halted until the Arkansas Archaeology Survey team conducted their investigation of the site on April 9, 2019. After peeling away layers of soil, the team realized that this was Dr. Baker's lost dump site, containing bottles, medical specimen jars and surgical tools that had been removed before the current owners took possession of the property. A number of these bottles appear to have been the same ones eyewitnesses reported seeing in Baker's morgue and autopsy rooms. General Manager Jack V. Moyer plans on exhibiting many of these objects in a special display in the morgue.

THE TOWN THAT WAS BROUGHT BACK TO LIFE BY THE DEAD

Senoia, Georgia

The little town of Senoia, Georgia, is located approximately twenty-five miles south of Atlanta. According to the legend, Senoia was named for a Creek Indian princess named Senoyah Heneha. She was the mother of Chief William McIntosh. Her husband was Captain William McIntosh Sr., a trader from Scotland. On February 12, 1825, Chief McIntosh and several other Creek Indian chiefs signed the Treaty of Indian Springs, essentially ceding all of the Creek lands to the State of Georgia. However, the Upper Creek tribes were so unhappy with the treaty that they burned McIntosh's house in Whitesburg, Georgia. Chief McIntosh and another Indian chief escaped the flames, but they were gunned down as they tried to flee. Two

Chartered in 1866, the railroad town of Senoia received a new lease on life in 2010 when the television series *The Walking Dead* began filming there. *Alan Brown*.

years later, the State of Georgia established a land lottery that included the region that now includes the town of Senoia. A large number of settlers began moving into the area in 1828. The date of the founding of Senoia is usually given as 1860, the year when Reverend Francis Warren Baggarly acquired the plot of land on which the town now sits. Later that year, tracks were laid for the Savannah, Griffin and North Alabama Railroad, which laid out the grid pattern for the town's streets in exchange for the property. For years, cotton and peaches were shipped out on the railroad. Until the mid-twentieth century, most of the goods that were shipped into Senoia came by rail. The City of Senoia was not officially chartered, though, until 1866. The old Rock House, which was used as a lodge hall and later as a storage warehouse and the Senoia Methodist Church, is believed to have originally served as an Indian trading post in the 1800s. One of the town's earliest entrepreneurs was C.F. Hollberg Sr., who opened a general store in 1894 and a pharmacy in 1909. By the 1950s, his holdings included dry goods, a grocery store, a hardware store, a pharmacy and a soda fountain. C. Frank "Buddy" Hollberg III converted his grandfather's business into a furniture store. The upstairs floors of Hollberg's store housed the Telegraph College of Senoia from the 1890s until 1907. At one time, Senoia had three banks, four active churches, four daily passenger trains, a cannery, three cotton gins and a Model T taxi service. Until well into the twentieth century, Senoia was a typical small southern town where people swapped tales on the front porch and listened to band concerts in the summertime.

By the end of the twentieth century, Senoia's glory days had passed, as was the case with many nineteenth-century railroad towns. However, everything changed in 1989 when Paul Lombardi began his search for the site of a new film studio. He decided to build in Georgia because it had good weather and diverse filming locations. Also, it was cheaper to film in Georgia than it was in most of the other states. Paul Lombardi bought a large tract of land that was close to downtown Senoia and within driving distance from the Hartsfield-Jackson Atlanta International Airport. After successfully lobbying for tax incentives in Georgia, Lombardi and his nephew, Scott Tigchelaar of Raleigh Studios, bought twenty-two properties in downtown Senoia, which could pass for "Anytown USA."

The set of *The Walking Dead*, which includes this windmill, is surrounded by an iron barricade. *Alan Brown*.

Since 1989, several movies have been shot in Senoia, including *Driving Miss Daisy* (1989), *Fried Green Tomatoes* (1991), *Sweet Home Alabama* (2002), *Meet the Browns* (2008) and *Footloose* (2011). A number of television series have filmed here as well, such as *Drop Dead Diva (*2009–12). By far, the most successful television show to be filmed in Senoia is *The Walking Dead* (2010–present). Renamed Woodbury for the television show, Senoia is a refuge for the survivors of the zombie apocalypse. Over the years, some residents were paid to let the grass grow in their front lawns to give the town a post-apocalyptic feel. Traffic was closed on Main Street one summer for the filming of a battle scene. A number of fake buildings, such as a law firm and a bank, were erected. Thousands of tourists, known to locals as "Walker Stalkers," flock to Senoia for its souvenir shops, zombie-themed businesses (such as a coffee shop called the Waking Dead) and its walking tours to sites where *The Walking Dead* has been filmed. During filming, the 250 people hired by Raleigh Studios shop and dine in Senoia, contributing significantly to the town's income. In fact, some store owners claim that profits rise by 30 percent when the film crews come to town. Scott Tigchelaar's development company, Senoia Enterprises, has restored restaurants, shops and bars to their nineteenth-century appearance. Thanks to the publicity brought to the town by the film company, Senoia's population has doubled to 2,000, proof that urban resurrection really is possible.

THE VERANDA'S PERMANENT GUESTS

Senoia, Georgia

In the early 1890s, businessman C.F. Hollberg Sr. moved to Senoia, Georgia. He began with a jewelry store, but before long, he began selling furniture in the same location. In 1894, Hollberg opened Hollberg's Fine Furniture. Around the same time, Hollberg bult a warehouse a couple of streets behind the furniture store. In 1906, he learned that the Savannah, Griffin & North Alabama Railroad and the Central of Georgia Railroad were going to converge in Senoia. To take advantage of the imminent influx of visitors to the little town, he built the Veranda Hotel on the slab of the warehouse. One of the Veranda's most illustrious guests was William Jennings Bryan, who stayed in room 1. Today, the Veranda is a stylish bed-and-breakfast that has served as a "home away from home" for a number of film crew members

Built in 1906, the Veranda is now a popular bed-and-breakfast. Its most haunted rooms, according to guests, are room 2 and room 5. *Alan Brown.*

and actors associated with *The Walking Dead* television series and other film projects.

According to the current owners, Rick and Laura Reynolds, the Veranda has a paranormal past. For years, Mrs. Hollberg held séances in room 2 to the left of the front door. Laura Reynolds said that a lady who dabbled in ghost hunting stayed in room 7 one night. Using two flashlights, the woman communicated with the ghosts: "She asked one of the spirits if it liked Laura, and it answered 'No.'" However, the most haunted room in the bed-and-breakfast is undoubtedly room 5. In the late 2000s, a woman who stayed in room 5 complained that someone moved furniture around during the night. A few years later, a couple who spent the night in the room directly below room 5—room 2—told the Reynolds the next morning that it sounded like a party was going on in room 5. People walking past room 5 have heard someone knocking on the door from the inside. These stories become even more unsettling when one realizes that room 5 is empty much of the time.

The Reynoldses' grandson, Austin, who lives at the Veranda, had his own ghostly encounter inside the historic home in 2016:

It was 5:45 p.m. I was sitting in the TV room on the first floor, doing my homework, when I started hearing noises upstairs, like people opening and closing doors and walking around. I was the only one inside the house at the time—my grandparents were on vacation, and no guests had checked in. I assumed that Sophia, the maid, was cleaning on the second floor, so I kept on reading until it sounded like someone was walking down the stairway. I expected to see Sophia standing at the bottom of the stairs with her cleaning supplies, but no one was there. I was so scared—it felt like I was frozen. I couldn't move. After a couple of minutes, I ran upstairs to my room. I stayed there all night long. Grandpa said it was just squirrels in the attic.

My wife and I stayed in room 5 in July 2018, but nothing unusual happened during the night. Rick Reynolds maintains a healthy skepticism when it comes to the ghosts in the Veranda. "If there are ghosts here, they're nice. My wife and I have never been scared here."

HELL'S GATE BRIDGE

Oxford, Alabama

Gephyrophobia is the fear of bridges. This phobia is not entirely irrational because many bridges in America are on the verge of collapse, especially in rural areas that lack the funds to maintain them properly. However, some bridges, especially those in remote locations, instill fear in the hearts of travelers because of the ghost stories that people tell about them. For example, spanning the Chunky River near Meridian, Mississippi, is an iron bridge built in 1850 called Stuckey's Bridge. It is named for a murderous innkeeper who was hanged from the bridge. His ghost has been seen hanging from the crossbeams. "Donkey Lady Bridge" near San Antonio is haunted by the ghost of a hideously burned woman whose family was murdered by the son of a wealthy merchant. An entirely different type of ghost story uses the Hell's Gate Bridge in Oxford, Alabama, as a backdrop.

After the one-lane truss bridge was built in the 1930s, people living in this once rural area used it to cross Choccolocco Creek as they traveled from parts of Oxford that lay north of the interstate at exit 188 to the southern parts. Despite the fact that the bridge resembles any number of iron bridges found in the Deep South, Hell's Gate Bridge stands out because of its name and its legends. For years, people bold enough to drive across the bridge at night spread the tale that when they looked over their shoulder, they could see the flames of hell engulfing the end of the bridge. The bridge's best-known ghost story concerns a young couple whose car drove off the bridge to their death in the 1950s. The story goes that people who have stopped their car on the bridge late at night and turned off their lights may detect a wet spot in the front passenger seat. Many believe that the ghost of the young lady who died in the creek tries to hitch a ride back to town when anyone parks on the bridge. Intrigued by the tales locals have been passing down about Hell's Gate Bridge for years, the Oxford Paranormal Society conducted a nighttime investigation of the bridge using voice recorders, a webcam and digital and 35mm cameras but were unable to collect any concrete evidence of the paranormal at the site.

Even though the bridge was becoming dilapidated, it remained open until 2002. Traffic is blocked off by massive cement blocks at both ends. Five "no trespassing" signs have been placed around the bridge to discourage thrill seekers. Today, the old bridge is sandwiched between the Choccolocco Park sports complex and the Commons shopping center. At the time of this writing, city officials in Oxford were debating whether or not to restore it or demolish it and replace it with a new bridge.

MYSTERIOUS FORT MOUNTAIN

Chatsworth, Georgia

Fort Mountain State Park is located in the Chattahoochee National Forest between Chatsworth and Ellijay, Georgia. It opened in 1936 on a 1,930-acre plot of land donated by Ivan Allen. The stone fire tower, the trails, the lake and a number of park buildings were constructed by the Civilian Conservation Corps, which operated as one of President Franklin Delano Roosevelt's New Deal programs between 1933 and 1942. With the help of state and federal funding in the 1990s, the park now includes 3,712 acres. Today, the park attracts bikers, hikers and horseback riders. In the spring and summer, Sand Beach is a big draw. The hardwood and pine forests add to the park's beauty, making it one of the most popular parks in the entire state.

However, Fort Mountain State Park is best known for the eighty-five-foot wall that zig-zags along the mountain's peak. The twelve-foot-thick wall varies in height from seven feet to two or three feet. It seems to have been built with stones taken from the summit. The wall is dotted with stone rings, cairns, twenty-nine pits and the ruins of a gateway. The origin of the wall is unknown. According to a 1962 archaeology report, the wall is of "prehistoric aboriginal construction." The park's historical marker, titled "Mystery Surrounds Fort Mountain," lists several possible explanations for the wall, including references to "sun worship and last-ditch defense by prehistoric white people, bloody warfare between Indian tribes, fortifications for Spanish conquistadors hunting gold and a honeymoon haven for Cherokee Indian newlyweds." Early settlers speculated that the wall was erected by Hernando de Soto as a defense against the Cherokee Indians around 1540. However, this theory was refuted in 1917 by a historian who noted that de Soto's visit to the area lasted only two weeks.

The best-known explanation can be found in the Cherokee legend of the "moon-eyed people," which was first presented in a book written by Benjamin Smith Barton in 1797. In the legend, the Cherokee recorded the arrival of a group of bearded, light-eyed white men who were small in stature. The Cherokee called them the "moon-eyed people" because they saw very well at night and poorly during the day. Before the Cherokee drove them out of the area, they built the wall and a temple containing a massive stone snake with ruby eyes. Some historians believe that this legend might actually refer to a Welsh prince named Madoc ab Owain Gwynedd. He fled his homeland in 1170 during a civil war created by the king's seven sons following his death and is said to have traveled to the area now known as Mobile Bay, Alabama, with his brother Rhirid and a few followers. After a few months, Madoc returned to Wales and recruited a larger force of explorers. They set sail for the New World and disappeared. Some people believe that Prince Madoc's explorers not only built the wall on Fort Mountain, but they also constructed similar fortifications near De Soto Falls, Alabama, and Chattanooga, Tennessee.

The mysterious origin of the wall has spawned several other legends. Visitors claim to have heard ghostly drumbeats in the night. People walking near the wall have also sighted ghost lights and spectral figures wearing bearskins. Because we will probably never know who built the wall, Fort Mountain will probably always be a legendary location.

THE BROWN MOUNTAIN LIGHTS

Burke County, North Carolina

The Brown Mountain Lights are among the most famous ghost lights in America. Eyewitnesses describe them as red, blue or green spheres that move erratically up and down. They can be seen from the Blue Ridge Parkway at mile posts 310 and 301. They can also be seen from North Carolina Highway 181, from the top of Table Rock outside of Morganton, from the Brown Mountain Overlook on NC Highway 181 between Morganton and Linville and from Wiseman's View four miles from Linville Falls. Close observation of the lights has proven to be elusive over the years because they vanish as one climbs the mountain.

The Brown Mountain Lights have spawned a number of legends. The earliest legend comes from the Cherokees, who observed the lights for centuries. They believed that the strange phenomenon was the result of a battle their ancestors fought with the Catawba Indians not far from Brown Mountain in AD 1200. The lights are the ghosts of the Cherokee women who combed the battlefield looking for the bodies of their sons, brothers and lovers. Another legend originated during the Revolutionary War. In the mid-eighteenth century, a family settled on a plot of land near Blowing Rock at the foot of Brown Mountain. After war broke out between the colonists and the British, the father left his wife and three children and went to war. When he returned, he was horrified to find that there was nothing left of his home but a few charred timbers. Half-crazed with grief, he began a frantic search for his loved ones. People said that his search extended well into the night. For weeks, his torch could be seen flickering about the mountain. Following his death, his ghost continues its nightly search for his family. Two of the mountain's best-known legends come from the nineteenth century. In 1850, a man was implicated in the disappearance of his wife. Search parties looking for any trace of the woman reported seeing bright lights flitting around the ridges and valleys. Years later, a skeleton found under a cliff was identified as that of the man's wife. According to an even more famous legend, a planter who went hunting in the mountains late one evening never returned. His family sent his most trustworthy slave to look for his master in the gorge, but he never returned either. People living around Brown Mountain claim that the glow of the faithful slave's lantern can still be seen at night as he continues his search.

Scientific studies have been conducted in and around Brown Mountain since the eighteenth century. A German cartographer and engineer named John William Geraud wrote about seeing the lights in an entry made in his journal in 1771. In a report issued in 1913, a U.S. Geological Study said that train headlights were misidentified as ghost lights. In 1919, Dr. W.J. Humphries of the U.S. Weather Bureau compared the Brown Mountain Lights to a similar phenomenon that has been observed in the Andes Mountains in South America for many years. A 1922 geological study submitted by H.C. Martin traced the source of the lights to fires, train headlights or different types of stationary lights. Critics of these two reports cite the appearance of the Brown Mountain Lights in 1916 after a flood destroyed houses and halted vehicular traffic in the area. Hobert A. Whitman analyzed soil and rocks from the mountain in 1940 and concluded that the lights were not generated by the region's geography. Using a 500,000-candlepower arc light on a peak twenty-two miles east of Brown Mountain, the Oak Ridge Isochronous Observation Network (ORION) noted that the light's red-orange glow was similar to the light sighted on Brown Mountain. Therefore, the Brown Mountain Lights could have been reflections of light bulbs and other types of artificial light. More modern theories include methane gas, moonshine stills, glowing emissions from decaying wood and even aliens who have set up a base on top of Brown Mountain. Writing in the *Skeptical Inquirer*, Joe Nickell said, "There is no single explanation because there is no single phenomenon. Just as we know that not all UFOs are weather balloons, not all Brown mountain lights have a single cause."

MISSISSIPPI'S SINGING RIVER

Pascagoula, Mississippi

The Pascagoula River is approximately 80 miles long. It drains an area of 8,800 square miles in the southeastern United States. Today, it remains the largest undammed river in the contiguous forty-eight states. The area is home to 327 species of birds that thrive in the nearby swamps and bayous. Some of the more fanciful of the visitors to the river believe that the distinctive singing sounds resonating around the river are not produced by the birds.

The Pascagoula people were part of a loosely connected band of Indians who lived along rivers in Mississippi and Louisiana. Because Pascagoula is the Choctaw word for "bread eater," they are thought to have been affiliated with the Choctaw Indians. The Pascagoula tribes were heavily influenced by other tribes and by the French and Spanish explorers between the sixteenth and eighteenth centuries.

According to legend, one of the tribes the Pascagoula interacted with was the Biloxi. Relations between the two tribes were harmonious until the chief of the Pascagoula, Altama, fell in love with the Biloxi princess Anola. However, she was already betrothed to the chief of Biloxi. Altama and Anola's insistence that they be allowed to marry instigated a war between the two tribes. The Biloxi made attacks on the Pascagoulas' village, killing a large number of them and forcing others into slavery. The survivors of these attacks made a fateful decision. Instead of dying in a battle in which they were vastly outnumbered or spending the remainder of their lives as slaves, the entire tribe decided to commit suicide. Driven by the conviction that they would be reunited in the afterlife, men, women and children held hands and walked into the Pascagoula River while singing their death song. Over the years, people have said that one can still hear the ghosts of the Pascagoula Indians as they march into the river. Scientists have offered a number of explanations for the strange sounds that occasionally emanate from the river, but none of them has proven to be true.

STUCKEY BRIDGE

Meridian, Mississippi

In 1847, Lauderdale County officials signed a contract to build a bridge across the Chunky River. Construction was completed in 1850. In 1901, the old bridge was dismantled, and a 112-foot-long truss bridged was erected on the site. Stuckey Bridge is known for its unique construction style and for its ghost stories.

The legend of Stuckey Bridge begins with the infamous Dalton Gang, who left behind a gang member named Stuckey in Lauderdale County, Mississippi, in the 1840s. Stuckey went on to build an inn on the banks of the Chunky River, which was heavily traveled by flatboats on their way to Meridian, Mississippi. At night, he stood on the riverside and signaled to the boats laden with goods to stop at his inn. Then he sneaked into guests' rooms, killed them and buried them along the river. Afterward, he laid claim

According to legend, an outlaw and innkeeper known only as Stuckey was hanged from this bridge in the late nineteenth century for murdering and robbing at least twenty of his guests. *Dudemanfellabra.*

to their possessions. In 1850, the sheriff of Lauderdale County decided to investigate the rumors that travelers on the Chunky River were disappearing. He organized a posse and rode out to Stuckey's inn. Stuckey was arrested and hanged from the trusses of the newly constructed bridge spanning the Chunky River. The story goes that when a new iron bridge was built on the Chunky River half a century later, workmen discovered several skeletons buried along the riverbank.

Stories of Stuckey's ghost date back to the nineteenth century. Some of the young people who have ventured out to the bridge to party at night claim to have seen the figure of an old man walking along the banks of the Chunky River, holding a lantern. Others claim to have heard Stuckey's body hitting the water under the bridge after being cut from the noose. People bold enough to gaze into the water after hearing the splash have seen an eerie glow hovering over the spot where Stuckey's body sank into the river.

Like most legends, this one does not hold up to close scrutiny. No outlaw connected with the Dalton Gang was named Stuckey. Also, Stuckey could not have been hanged from the trusses because the truss bridge was not constructed until 1901. Apparently, the people of Lauderdale County are unwilling to let the truth get in the way of a good story.

THE CAVES OF LOOKOUT MOUNTAIN

Chattanooga, Tennessee

The caves of Lookout Mountain will be forever connected with a local caver named Leo Lambert (1895–1955). Lambert was a chemist who moved to Chattanooga to be close to his fiancée, Ruby Eugenia Losey. He married her in 1916. In 1923, Lambert's company, the Lookout Mountain Cave Company, purchased land above Lookout Mountain Cave, which had been used by Native Americans, outlaws and Confederate and Union troops. The natural entrance to the cave had been sealed by the Southern Railway, so Lambert decided to make a new opening higher up the mountain and eventually conduct tours through the cave. In 1928, he began drilling an elevator shaft into the cave. After finally discovering a void in the rock, he and his business associates squeezed into a crevice 18 inches high and 5 feet wide. They were amazed to find a 145-foot waterfall 260 feet inside the mountain. Lambert named the waterfall after his wife, Ruby Falls. The elevator shaft finally reached the original cave after ninety-two days of drilling. Once Lambert had installed the elevator and prepared walking paths, the cave was open to the public in 1929. The Lookout Mountain Cave Company declared bankruptcy during the Great Depression and was taken over by new owners.

Today, Lookout Mountain Cave is a popular tourist attraction. Beginning in late September and running through October is the "haunted cavern" event called "Dread Hallow." The possibility that the cave might be haunted was suggested years before by a legend about a caver named Lomax. He was hired to explore the cave and bring out whatever treasures might be hidden there. Making his way through a narrow passage, he found a large chamber and several small chambers. He was walking through one of the small chambers when his lantern went out. Unable to see anything at all, Lomax lost all sense of direction. After a few hours, a search party was organized to find Lomax. After several hours, they found the signs he had carved on the cave walls marking his way. When they finally found him sitting in one of the small chambers, he was unable to speak. As the men led him out of the cave, he warned them about going deeper into the cave. He was immediately taken to a hospital. Sitting up in his bed, he told his friends and family that he would never enter the cave again. Although he never explained what had happened to him, it was obvious that he had had some sort of traumatic experience in the cave because his hair had turned

Left: Ruby Falls is a 145-foot waterfall 260 feet inside Lookout Mountain Cave. A local caver named Leo Lambert named the falls after his wife, Ruby. *Alan Brown*.

Below: Visitors to Raccoon Mountain Caverns have photographed a number of orbs hovering around this strange rock formation known as the "shield." *Alan Brown*.

completely white. Some people believe Lomax had encountered the spirits of people who had gotten lost years before and left their bones in the cave.

A year after Lambert discovered Ruby Falls, he was invited by several local farmers to explore a different cave on Lookout Mountain. Lambert crawled through a tight opening in a horizontal crevice and found himself in a cave that had previously been unexplored. He spent the next two years walking through a network of trails throughout the cave before opening to the general public on June 28, 1931. In 1951, the new managers of the cave—the Smith brothers—crawled through a small hole in the Crystal Palace Room and eventually came out in a much larger room. The route they took is now known as the Crystal Palace Tour. In the late 1970s, the name of the caverns was changed from Tennessee Caverns to Raccoon Mountain Cave Tours.

According to Amy Petulla in the book *Haunted Chattanooga*, the caverns are haunted by the ghost of a night watchman named Willie Cowan. Each night, he routinely strolled through the gift shop and subterranean passages while smoking pipes and cigars. His love of tobacco proved to be fatal. On November 30, 1966, Willie fell asleep while smoking a cigar, which ignited the gift shop. The flames quickly consumed the gift shop and spread to the power plant. Willie was incinerated in the flames. Ever since Willie died in the cave fire, his spirit has tried to make its presence known. A number of tour guides have heard spectral whistling sounds and detected the aromatic odor of pipe and cigar smoke in the cave. The smell of carbide, which was used in lanterns years ago, also wafts through the cave on occasion. Amy Petulla reports that one of the tour guides actually witnessed Willie's full-body apparition standing near Headache Rock, not far from the entrance to the cave. One of the owners, Bob Perlapis, saw Willie's ghost wearing his trademark red flannel shirt near the second Wild Cave entrance. Many visitors have captured orbs in their photographs of the Cave Shield, which hangs from the top of the cave without any of the sides touching the rest of the cave. Visitors who use their imagination can see the image of a coat of arms on the face of the shield.

PETIT JEAN MOUNTAINS

Conway County, Arkansas

Petit Jean Mountain is the largest of a line of mountains that vary from 900 feet to 1,200 feet above sea level and stretch 5.5 miles from east to west and 2.6 miles from north to south. Geologists believe that the top of the mountain was once a giant valley. Archaeologists have uncovered evidence of Native American habitations on the mountain dating back ten thousand years, including rock art on the cliff face. White explorers traveling along the confluence of the Petit Jean River with the Arkansas River took note of the mountainous grandeur surrounding them. Author Washington Irving was particularly entranced by the mountain when he visited it in 1832: "Petit Jean Mountain—a picturesque line on the Arkansas highlands—of mingled rock and cliff below." The origin story behind the mountain's name is as romantic as Irving's description of it.

Legend has it that sometime in the 1700s, a French girl named Adrienne Dumont dressed like a boy to follow her boyfriend America. Her lover—referred to as Cheves, Chavet and Jean-Jacques Chavez in the variants—is thought to have been a member of an exploratory expedition. Some people say Adrienne's lover was in a hurry to leave France because he had killed King Louis XVI's favorite nephew. In one variant, she followed him to get revenge for his having deserted her. In most of the versions, "Petit Jean," as the sailors called Adrienne, contracted a fatal disease after nursing her husband back to health. In some accounts, her true identity is discovered while she is dying. In other versions, she voluntarily reveals her true identity to her love just before she dies. In all of the variants, the girl's body is buried on the top of the mountain that bears her name.

The Petit Jean Mountains are named after Adrienne Dumont, who dressed like a boy named "Petit Jean" to follow her lover to America. *ErgoSum88*.

WITCH DANCE

Houston, Mississippi

Located on the Natchez Trace Parkway at milepost 232.2, Witch Dance is a bicycle-only campground. It also serves as a staging area for the Witch Dance horse trail. The National Park Service sign at the entrance to the campground provides a capsulized version of the legend that gives rise to the site's name.

The first inhabitants in the Witch Dance area were bands of Paleo Indians connected to the Hopewell culture. They chose this particular place because a medicine stick the leader was carrying in their search for a new home pointed straight up. According to the legend, witches familiar with the area's supernatural overtones began holding their nocturnal ceremonies here, which involved dancing and feasting all night. It is said that grass would not grow in the places where the witches' feet touched the ground.

Over time, Witch Dance acquired a sinister reputation. The Choctaw and Chickasaw Indians gave the cursed spot a wide berth, as did most of the whites traveling on the Natchez Trace. One of these men paid a heavy price for desecrating the site. An outlaw named Big Harpe, who terrorized the Natchez Trace with his brother Little Harpe, laughed when his Indian guide told him the story of Witch Dance and jumped from one bare spot to the next. This proved to be a serious mistake. A posse tracked Big Harpe down in August 1799 near Witch Dance. A man whose wife and baby had been brutally murdered by Big Harpe slowly cut off the outlaw's head while he was still alive. The man then nailed Big Harpe's skull to a tree. A few weeks later, an old woman who was said to be a witch removed Big Harpe's skull and ground it into power.

Today, many of the scorched places at Witch Dance are covered with kudzu and difficult to find. Nevertheless, people still claim to hear cackling laughter and muffled drumming sounds. Some sensitive visitors claim to have felt as if they were being watched by a pair of unseen eyes. The witches may be gone, but Witch Dance is still a spooky place, especially at night.

THE GURDON LIGHT

Clark County, Arkansas

The Gurdon light is a mysterious light that that has frightened and intrigued the residents of Clark County, Arkansas, for generations. The phenomenon's backstory sounds familiar to anyone who has knowledge of any of the South's ghost lights. A railroad worker who was walking the tracks outside of town tripped on one of the railroad ties and fell in the path of an oncoming train. The next day, the man's decapitated corpse was found lying across the tracks. His head was nowhere to be found. Supposedly, the light that hundreds of people have seen floating along the tracks is the glow of the lantern held by the railroad worker as he searches for his missing head. This story differs from the other "Phantom Brakeman" stories in that it was generated shortly after a real-life murder was committed in Gurdon.

Residents of Gurdon say that the light can be seen by parking off the road and walking two and a half miles past the railroad trestles. The best place to see the light is toward the top of a long hill. Eyewitnesses describe the light as being a blue ball with a distinct border. The light sways back and forth and never stops moving. The best time to see the light is under cloudy and overcast conditions. Because the light has been sighted far away from any roads, it is unlikely that it is actually the reflection of the headlights from passing cars.

MOSS MOUNTAIN FARM

Roland, Arkansas

Thomas Nuttall (January 5, 1786–September 10, 1859) was an English botanist and zoologist who achieved fame for the expeditions he made in America from 1810 until 1841. He traveled to the Great Lakes in 1810. The next year, he was a member of the Astor expedition up the Missouri River collecting plants previously unknown to science. From 1818 to 1820, Nuttall studied the flora along the Arkansas and Red River. He published his findings in his *Journal of Travels into the Arkansas Territory* during the year 1819. He left behind a mystery that is still passed down today.

Moss Mountain Farm is an estate owned by television host, conservationist and author P. Allen Smith. With its breathtaking view of the Arkansas River and its beautiful rose gardens, Smith's farm has become a popular venue for weddings and special events. It is also the setting for a blood-curdling legend. In 1819, Thomas Nuttall and his three flatboats were headed west on the Arkansas River when he decided to spend the night on Beaver Island, a large island in the middle of the river. During the night of October 31, all of the crew, including the watchman, fell asleep, probably because the island's isolated location gave the illusion of security.

Nuttall awoke the next morning to a scene of horror. All but four members of his party had been murdered during the night. Because of the mutilated condition of the bodies, the men concluded that their friends had been killed by a pack of wild animals. Nuttall, however, did not accept the easy explanation because he saw what appeared to be human figures walking through the camp at night. The spirits responsible for the heinous crime have been said to come back up the river every Halloween night.

MARFA LIGHTS

Marfa, Texas

The Marfa lights are an aerial phenomenon that has been observed near U.S. Route 67 on Mitchell Flat east of Marfa, Texas. *Coronet* magazine published the first account of the ghost lights in the July 1957 issue. Elton Miles's book *Tales of the Big Bend* (1976) included sightings dating to the nineteenth century. The earliest reported sighting occurred in March 1883. A rancher named Robert Reed Ellison was herding cattle across the Marfa plain when he observed the strange lights. Two years later, Joe and Anne Humphreys had their own sightings. In his book *Strange Lights in West Texas* (2009), author James Bunnell lists thirty-four sightings of the Marfa lights. To accommodate the influx of visitors to Marfa, Texas, a view park was created on the south side of U.S. Route 90 approximately nine miles east of Marfa. According to the marker erected by the Texas Historical Commission, the Marfa lights change colors, fluctuate in intensity and move about. No one can predict when the lights will appear.

A number of theories had been offered to explain the Marfa lights. Native Americans believed that the lights were fallen stars. For years,

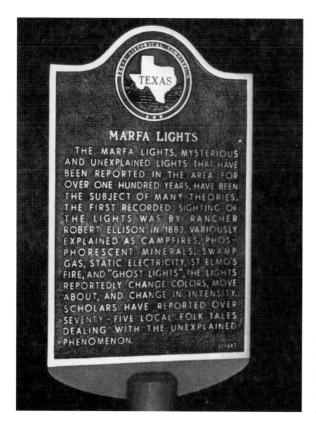

MARFA LIGHTS

THE MARFA LIGHTS, MYSTERIOUS AND UNEXPLAINED LIGHTS THAT HAVE BEEN REPORTED IN THE AREA FOR OVER ONE HUNDRED YEARS, HAVE BEEN THE SUBJECT OF MANY THEORIES. THE FIRST RECORDED SIGHTING OF THE LIGHTS WAS BY RANCHER ROBERT ELLISON IN 1883. VARIOUSLY EXPLAINED AS CAMPFIRES, PHOSPHORESCENT MINERALS, SWAMP GAS, STATIC ELECTRICITY, ST. ELMO'S FIRE, AND "GHOST LIGHTS", THE LIGHTS REPORTEDLY CHANGE COLORS, MOVE ABOUT, AND CHANGE IN INTENSITY. SCHOLARS HAVE REPORTED OVER SEVENTY-FIVE LOCAL FOLK TALES DEALING WITH THE UNEXPLAINED PHENOMENON.

Sightings of the Marfa lights near U.S. Route 67 on Mitchell Flat east of Marfa, Texas, date back to the nineteenth century. *ADSCN3737.*

observers have suggested that the lights were swamp gas or St. Elmo's Fire. Phosphorescent minerals could also be responsible for the phenomenon. Most scientists believe that the lights are a mirage produced by sharp temperature gradients between cold and warm layers of air. Because the lights from cars parked on U.S. 67 were visible from the view park, investigators from the Society of Physics at the University of Texas–Dallas concluded that the lights were most likely produced by the headlights from cars riding along U.S. 67 between Marfa and Presidio, Texas. Some of the sightings, like those dating to the nineteenth century, could have been campfires. Still, no one can explain why the lights tend to vanish when someone approaches them. Could it be, as some say, that the lights are the spirits of the Indians who lived in this area centuries ago or the ghosts of Spanish conquistadors?

DEVIL'S TRAMPING GROUND

Bear Creek, North Carolina

Located ten miles from Siler City is the Devil's Tramping Ground, a path approximately twelve inches wide that forms a perfect circle forty feet in diameter. Grass, weeds, wildflowers and trees grow in abundance outside of the circle, but nothing grows on the ring-shaped track. This phenomenon has given rise to several legends, the most prominent of which holds that Satan walks the path at night, lost in thought as he ponders different ways to ensnare humanity. Supposedly, the devil's hoofprints have scorched the earth, making it infertile. It is said that objects like twigs and rocks or even transplanted grass placed on the path are either brushed aside or missing. People living in the area claim that hunting dogs shy away from the strange path with their tails tucked between their legs.

Superstitious settlers traveling to North Carolina gave the Devil's Tramping Ground its name in the early 1800s. However, some scholars believe that the area served as an ancient meeting place where Native American tribes conducted their ceremonies. In another Indian legend, a tribal chief named Croatan was buried here following a battle. He was so highly esteemed by the gods that they transformed the site into a permanent memorial to Croatan, whose name was carved on a tree by members of the Lost Colony of Roanoke Island.

Scientists have presented several theories to explain that barren track of land. Those familiar with the agricultural history of the area have suggested that the circular path was made by horses used in the operations of an old

Early settlers named this perfect circle "The Devil's Tramping Ground" because nothing will grow there. *Jason Horne.*

molasses mill. Scientists from the North Carolina Department of Agriculture used samples of earth taken from the path to form the most plausible theory. Tests conducted on the samples indicated that the ground has a very high salt content, which would prevent any vegetation from growing.

In recent years, the Devil's Tramping Ground has attracted its share of curiosity seekers and partiers, who have littered the ground with empty beer bottles, cigarette butts and cans. Like many out-of-the-way places with an "evil" reputation, the Devil's Tramping Ground has become popular with young people intent upon proving their courage or testing the validity of the legend. Their presence has probably scared away the devil, who now finds it difficult to concentrate in the midst of so much revelry.

THREE-LEGGED LADY ROAD

Columbus, Mississippi

Nash Road in Columbus, Mississippi, is located not far from the lock and dam. It has acquired the nickname "Three-Legged Lady Road" because of sightings that have occurred between 2661–4548 Nash Road. A number of different legends have been generated at this location, all of which attempt to explain how the woman acquired the extra limb. In one of the variants, a young girl was murdered and dismembered at the site of an old church on Nash Road that has long since been torn down. All her mother found was a severed leg. She was so overcome with grief that her mind became unhinged, and she sewed the leg onto her own body so that the girl would always be with her.

In another version of the tale, a poor farmer discovered that his wife had been unfaithful to him with a Civil War veteran. The farmer murdered her lover and threw his corpse off a bridge on Nash Road. As the body fell, one of its legs was ripped from its body. When the farmer's wife found out what had happened, she went insane. She sewed her lover's leg onto her own body and killed her husband. Then she committed suicide.

In a reverse version of the story, a woman living on Nash Road discovered that her husband had a girlfriend on the side. She shot him and amputated one of his legs. She sewed it onto her body so that he would never leave her. She then buried the rest of his body in the cemetery. When the congregation of the church on Nash Road accused her of killing her husband, she locked all of the doors during Sunday services and burned up the church, along with all of the church members.

In one final version, a young girl named Rose was sacrificed and dismembered by Satanists in the woods along Nash Road. Her mother became so distraught that she lost her mind. She can still be seen today walking along Nash Road at night, cradling her daughter's leg in her arms. In a variant of the tale, she sewed the girl's leg onto her own body.

All of the variants end the same way. Anyone curious—or foolish enough—to travel on Nash Road in the hopes of seeing the Three-Legged Lady should stop in the middle of the road near the site of the old church. After the driver honks the horn three times, the Three-Legged Lady knocks on the roof of the car, signifying that the race is on. She then races the car to the end of the road, slamming her body against the car doors the entire way.

THE GEORGIA GUIDESTONES

Elberton, Georgia

In 1969, a tall, well-dressed stranger calling himself R.C. Christian hired the Elberton Granite Finishing Company to build a monument north of the city of Elberton off U.S. Highway 77. The monument would stand 19 feet, 3 inches tall and would be made from granite slabs weighing 237,746 pounds. The stones would be placed at an elevation of 750 feet above sea level approximately 90 miles east of Atlanta, 45 miles from Athens, Georgia, and 9 miles from the center of Elberton. Christian told Joe Fendley of Elberton Granite that the stones would serve as a clock, a compass and an astronomical calendar. Christian presented Fendley with a scale wooden model of the guidestones and ten pages of specifications. Before leaving the office, Christian explained that he was part of a group of people who had been planning this project for over twenty years. Christian asked that all plans be destroyed after the monument was finished and that all personal information about him be withheld from the public. He purchased the five-acre site from a farmer named Wayne Mullinex, who was permitted to graze his cattle around the monument. The president of the Granite City Bank, Wyatt C. Martin, handled the finances. Martin was instructed never to reveal Christian's real name. The people involved in the business transaction were led to believe that Christian had unlimited funds.

The massive monument was unveiled on March 22, 1980, in a cow pasture before a crowd estimated in size between one hundred and four hundred people. The five guidestones were topped by a capstone weighing nearly 240,000 pounds. Over four thousand letters were etched into the stone. The monument is inscribed in eight different languages: English, Spanish, Swahili, Hindi, Hebrew, Arabic, Chinese and Russian. The names of four ancient languages—Classical Greek, Babylonian cuneiform, Sanskrit and Egyptian hieroglyphics—are inscribed at the top. A mystery hovers around a time capsule that—according to an instructional tablet—was buried at the site; however, the date when the capsule is to be opened is omitted. Two of the monument's odd astronomical features is a hole in the capstone that acts as a solar calendar at noon and a slot enabling the viewer to watch the sun rise during the summer or winter solstice. Three of the monument's ten edicts include the following:

Maintain humanity under 500,000,000 in perpetual balance with nature.
Rule passion-faith-tradition—and all things with tempered reason.
Be not a cancer on the earth—Leave room for nature.

The Georgia Guidestones have been steeped in controversy since they were first erected in 1980. The monument has been linked by conspiracy theorists to the New World Order, a shadowy group espousing a totalitarian one-world government because of commandments such as "Guide reproduction wisely—improving fitness and diversity." Some fundamentalists believe that the monument is the work of Satan. In 2008, vandals defaced the guidestones with polyurethane paint and graffiti, such as "Death to the new world order."

13

UNIVERSITY LEGENDS

THE TUTWILER HALL MASSACRE

Tuscaloosa, Alabama

Michel de Nostradame was born in Saint Remy-de-Provence in 1503. He was tutored by his maternal grandfather, Jean de St. Remy, at an early age. Nostradame enrolled at the University of Avignon to study medicine at age fourteen. He began his career as a physician healing victims of the bubonic plague. In 1525, he Latinized his name from Nostradame to Nostradamus, as many physicians did at this time. After marrying a rich widow, Anne Ponsarde, in 1547, he began studying the occult in earnest, spending hours late at night creating self-induced trances by staring into a bowl filled with water and herbs. Nostradamus published his first book of predictions for the coming year in 1550. By 1554, he had embarked on a ten-volume collection of one hundred predictions forecasting the next two thousand years. The first volume in the series, *The Prophecies*, was published in 1555. To avoid religious persecution, Nostradamus obscured the meaning of his prophecies by writing them in quatrains and by incorporating a mixture of Greek, Latin and Italian. Some of the predictions he wrote prior to his death on July 1, 1556, are believed to have accurately predicted future events, such as the rise of Adolf Hitler, the atomic bomb and the destruction of the Twin Towers in New York on 9/11. One of his lesser-known predictions is said to concern the University of Alabama in Tuscaloosa, Alabama. Supposedly, Nostradamus predicted that on Halloween night, sometime between the 1960s and the 1990s, a number of female students living in Tutwiler Hall would be bludgeoned to death. The only clues in the prophecy linking it to Tutwiler Hall at the University of Alabama is that the dormitory was located close to a cemetery and a mental asylum.

The truth is that a cemetery is located on the northeastern edge of the campus of the University of Alabama. The first person buried at the University of Alabama Cemetery was a student who died in 1839. His family eventually relocated the young man's remains to a cemetery closer to home. On July 6, 1844, another student, William J. Crawford, was interred there. He was followed by two slaves: Jack, a slave owned by the university, and William, a seven-year-old boy belonging to President Manly. After the Pratt family acquired part of the property, they buried some of their family members there. Today, the graves of William Crawford and the two slaves are memorialized by a marker on Hackberry Lane.

Tutwiler Hall is also fairly close to a former mental hospital. Bryce Hospital was founded in 1859 as the Alabama Insane Hospital. It was named after the first superintendent, Peter Bryce, who instituted the moral treatment plan at the hospital. Bryce believed that patient work was an important factor in the treatment of mental health. In 2010, the former hospital and grounds were purchased by the University of Alabama, which intends to convert the old buildings into a welcome center, museums and a center for performing arts.

Although these two clues seem, on the surface, to point to Tutwiler Hall as the site of the massacre, the fact remains that scholars have found no concrete evidence of such a prophecy in the prophet's quatrains. However, the absence of historical verification of the prophecy has not affected the legend's durability in any tangible way. In the November 2, 2007 edition of the University of Alabama's student newspaper, the *Crimson*, staff reporter Martha Gravlee wrote, "On Wednesday night, female students strolled out of Julia Tutwiler Hall in groups of five and six. Some carried only purses, and some had a change of clothes draped over their arms. A few even carried overnight bags." Gravlee added that the night passed "without havoc," but she refrained from speculating as to the reason why the students left the dormitory.

THE UNIVERSITY OF SOUTH CAROLINA'S THIRD-EYE MAN

Columbia, South Carolina

The University of South Carolina's signature ghost story focuses on a phantom known to students as the "Third-Eye Man." Supposedly, he is a denizen of the university's underground system of tunnels, which date to the 1880s. The tunnels could be accessed near the Riverfront Park, under Gervais Street Bridge and behind Colonial Life Arena.

Prior to 1949, the tunnel's legendary status rested primarily on the belief that some of the tunnels had been used during the Civil War. However, they acquired a much more sinister dimension when a student at the university named Christopher Nichols saw a weird man who appeared to be dressed in silver clothes lift up a manhole cover across the street from the Longstreet Theater, climb into the sewer portal and pull the cover back into position. Later, Nichols wrote about the "Sewer Man" in the student newspaper, the *Gamecock*.

Then on April 17, 1950, a university policeman was making his rounds when he found the mutilated carcass of a chicken on a loading dock behind the Longstreet Theater. At first, the officer assumed that the mutilation of the chicken was part of a fraternity prank. He walked over to his car and called in his find to the police station. When he returned to the loading dock, the officer was shocked to see a silver man crouched over the dead chicken. In the beam of his flashlight, he could make out the intruder's features—a grotesquely deformed face and what seemed to be a small third eye on the creature's forehead. Frantically, the officer ran back to his police car. By the time the other officers arrived, nothing was left of the chicken but a few scattered feathers. The strange creature was gone as well.

Stories of the "Third-Eye Man" proliferated in the 1960s and 1970s, when students held parties in the tunnels. One fall night, a group of fraternity brothers took three pledges down to the tunnels for an initiation ritual. They entered through the basement of Gambrell and headed west. They turned a corner, and the young men encountered what one of them described as "a crippled man dressed in silver." Without warning, the strange man charged the students with a lead pipe in his hand. He knocked a pledge named Matthew Tabor to the ground with the pipe. Two of the young men rushed to the police department to report the incident. The police searched the entire system of tunnels but found no trace of the "Third-Eye Man." Afterward, the police closed the entrances of the tunnels. A maintenance man who works at the university today said that staff does not use the tunnels unless it is "absolutely necessary."

SPIRIT LIFE AT THE UNIVERSITY OF VIRGINIA

Charlottesville, Virginia

Former president Thomas Jefferson founded the University of Virginia in 1819 as an institution "on the most extensive and liberal scale that our circumstances would call for and our faculties meet." The ideal university, from Jefferson's point of view, would be one in which religious doctrine and higher education would be separate. His new university also differed from others at the time in that instead of being able to major only in medicine, law or divinity, students could study mathematics, chemistry, ancient languages, modern languages, natural philosophy and moral philosophy. He insisted that a professor's theology should have no place in the institution. Today, the number of majors at UVA has grown to 121. Ironically, the university that once prided itself on offering courses that deemphasized religion now seems to celebrate its ghost stories.

The nickname of the building known as Pavilion VI—"The Romance Pavilion"—is a reference to its oldest legends. The first of these tales involves a romance between the beautiful daughter of a professor and a student of whom he did not approve. After her parents broke off the relationship, the young woman died of a broken heart. The story ends with the girl's mournful spirit walking the halls of the university. According to "Sandy" Gilliam, UVA historian, tour guides concocted this familiar-sounding story to explain the building's nickname. The truth, however, is much more mundane. It was called "The Romance Pavilion" because for fifty years, Romance languages were taught here.

A far less romantic legend concerns a professor who lived in Pavilion VI in the mid-nineteenth century. His wife loved her home so much that after her husband died, she placed his corpse in a chair by the window and changed his clothes daily to give the impression that he was still alive. The ruse worked for about a month.

During his one semester at the University of Virginia, Edgar Allan Poe lived at 131 West Range dormitory. A poem etched on a window in the room is credited to him. *American Bookmen*.

One of UVA's most famous students is a man normally associated with the uncanny. Edgar Allan Poe enrolled at UVA in 1826 and stayed only a single semester. During his short time at the university, Poe displayed an affinity for languages. He stayed at 131 West Range dormitory. For many years, a poem attributed by many to Poe was etched on a window in the room:

> *O Thou timid one, do not let thy*
> *Form slumber within these*
> *Unhallowed walls,*
> *For herein lies*
> *The ghost of an awful crime.*

The nature of the crime referred to in the poem has been a source of speculation for decades.

Named for UVA's first president, Edwin Alderman, the Alderman Library is reputed to be haunted by two spirits. One is the ghost of Dr. Bennett Wood Green, a Confederate surgeon whose large book collection was donated to the university following his death in 1913. The books were moved from the Rotunda to Alderman Library in 1938. Dr. Green's ghost, some say, attached itself to his books and followed them to their new home. Described as a short man with a long beard, his ghost has been sighted in the stacks and in the upper hallways after midnight. A different ghost haunts the Garnett Room, which houses books donated by the family of Muscoe Russell Hunter. The spirit haunting this room is said to be the ghost of an unnamed Garnett family physician who maintained the collection when the Garnett estate was abandoned

HENDERSON COLLEGE'S LADY IN BLACK

Arkadelphia, Arkansas

"The Lady in Black" is not only Henderson College's most beloved legend, but it is also Arkansas's best-known romantic ghost story. The story is told during freshman orientation, and sightings are most commonly reported during that time. Students are divided as to whether or not the ghost is real. Evidence suggests, though, that the story may be based on fact. As is true with many legends, several variants of the story exist, but the most important plot elements remain constant.

In the standard version of the tale, a Henderson football player risked being ostracized by dating a freshman at Henderson College's rival, Ouachita, named Jane. She was a religious young lady and one of the college's best biology students. Joshua finally yielded to peer pressure when he was criticized for dating a "science nerd." Joshua broke up with Jane and began dating a girl from Henderson, causing Jane to sink into a deep depression. Unable to cope with the death of her romance to the handsome football player, Jane donned a long, black dress and a black veil. She then walked to a cliff overlooking the Ouachita River and jumped off. "The Lady in Black" has been sighted for decades, usually during Homecoming. Eyewitnesses say that she seems to be looking for her lost love as she wanders around the campus. Many students have seen Jane's ghost walking in and out of the women's dormitory, possibly in an attempt to frighten the girl who took her place in Joshua's heart. Some residents claim to have heard Jane's mournful cries resounding throughout the dorm.

14

LEGENDARY MONSTERS AND PHANTOMS

THE WHITE RIVER MONSTER

Newport, Arkansas

The White River flows 722 miles through Arkansas and Missouri. It originates from the Boston Mountains of northwest Arkansas in the Ozark–St. Francis National Forest. The White River is impounded by a total of eight dams, the first of which, the Powersite Dam, formed Lake Taneycomo in 1913. The river is navigable once it reaches Batesville, Arkansas, in the Mississippi River Valley. The White River is known by anglers as one of the best trout fisheries in the entire United States. Rainbow, brown and cutthroat trout are commonly taken from the White River. For cryptozoologists, however, the river is intriguing because of the legend of the White River Monster.

The first sighting of the White River Monster occurred in Newport in the northeastern part of the state in 1915, when farmers observed a bizarre creature just off the banks. The next sighting occurred during the summer of 1937 when fishing had dropped off dramatically. On July 1, the owner of a riverside planation, Bramlett Bateman, caught sight of a beast that he described as being four or five feet wide by twelve feet long, with the face of a catfish and the skin of an elephant, lolling on the surface of the water. Bateman estimated that the beast was "as wide as a car and

Since 1915, fishermen reported seeing an aquatic monster, approximately twenty feet long with the face of a catfish and peeling skin. The Arkansas state legislature passed a law in 1973 protecting the monster. *Jpowersok at English Wikipedia.*

three cars long." Concerned that the monster would damage his crops, he had planned to blow it up with dynamite, but he was unable to secure permission from the authorities.

As word of the White River Monster's existence spread, people began flocking to the area in the hope of catching or killing the beast. Some of the visitors brought explosives, cameras and even a machine gun. Over one hundred sightings were reported at this time, probably because so many people were looking for it. When the number of sightings dwindled, people began talking about making a giant net to catch it in, but plans were halted by the lack of money and materials. A deep-sea diver searched for the beast in an eddy where it had been seen previously, but he found nothing even remotely resembling a monster. Rumors spread that the creature was just a hoax concocted by Bateman.

For over thirty years, nothing more was heard of the White River Monster. Then in 1971, the sightings resumed. One of the first eyewitnesses described it as being as big as a boxcar and having a horn protruding from its forehead.

Some people described it as being twenty feet long with smooth, peeling skin. Other claimed that it made weird noises, like the sound of a horse's neigh and a cow's moo. Even more convincing was the discovery of three-toed, fourteen-inch prints and crushed vegetation on Towhead Island.

In 1973, the Arkansas legislature passed a law creating the White River Monster Refuge along the White River, making it illegal to "molest, kill, trample, or harm the White River monster while he is in the retreat." Despite the fact that many visitors have been frightened by the beast, many locals are very fond of "Whitey," as it has come to be known.

THE POPE LICK MONSTER

Louisville, Kentucky

Legend tripping is an anthropological term pertaining to the practice of making pilgrimages to legendary sites where a supernatural or tragic event is reputed to have occurred. Frequently, these are remote places where adolescents test their courage as a sort of rite of passage. Because partying is often part of the legend tripping experience, many young people have been injured while visiting "murder mansions," "haunted bridges" or other mysterious locations. Legend tripping occurs all over the world, but it has been the most thoroughly documented in the United States. One of the most infamous of these sites is the Pope Lick train trestle in Louisville.

Among the world's human hybrid monsters, the best known are found in ancient Greek mythology. The legend of the Pope Lick Monster of Louisville, Kentucky, seems to have its roots in such mythological beasts as the centaurs (half-man/half-horse) and the Minotaur (half-man/half-bull). This large creature is said to have the upper body of a man and the lower torso of a goat or sheep with claw-like human hands, ivory-white skin and long, tangled hair. Ram-like horns or, some say, short, goat-like horns, protrude from its skull. The monster is said to use hypnosis or a siren-like voice to compel its victims to climb the train trestle and stand on the tracks. Its actual physical appearance is pure conjecture, however, because no confirmed sightings of the beast have been reported. The few eyewitnesses have caught just a glimpse of a weird shape running through the woods.

According to the most popular origin story, the Pope Lick Monster's beginnings can be traced back to Colonel Beauregard Schildnect, who was an unscrupulous ringmaster. Performers claimed that he abused them and stole from audience members and local homeowners. During one of the circus's trips through Maryland, Schildnect came into possession of a deformed child who bore the features of a human being and a goat. The ringmaster beat the child and imprisoned him in a cage when he put him on display. Because of the child's mistreatment, his hatred for people intensified. Legend has it that he made his escape during a thunderstorm after a bolt of lightning caused the circus train to derail. He viciously attacked and killed the few survivors, one of whom was Colonel Schildnect. Locals say that he continues to vent his rage on anyone foolish enough to venture into the Pope Lick Creek area. In a lesser-known variant of the tale, the monster is the reincarnation of a farmer who sacrificed goats in return for Satanic powers.

A number of legend trippers have endangered and, in some cases, lost their lives in an attempt to catch sight of the Pope Lick Monster while standing on top of the Pope Lick train trestle. Two of these thrill-seekers were Ohio tourists David Knee and his twenty-six-year-old girlfriend, Roquel Bain. They learned about the legend of the Pope Lick Monster on the internet and were inspired to put the creature's existence to the test in April 2016. After climbing a path bypassing the eight-foot-high fence surrounding the train trestle, the couple were standing on the 742-foot trestle when a train rumbled toward them at a high rate of speed. When the train was approximately 40 feet away, Knee jumped over the side of the bridge and clung to the metal edge with his arms and a single leg. His girlfriend was not so lucky. The train struck her head-on, knocking her 80 feet to the ground below. Despite the fact that the Norfolk Southern Railway has posted a large "No Trespassing" sign on the fence, more people are likely to die from falling off the trestle or from being hit by a train in an effort to see what is most likely a mythical creature.

THE PHANTOM OF BUNNYMAN BRIDGE

Clifton, Virginia

According to folklorist Harold Brunvand, urban legends "belong to the subclass of folk narratives, legends, that—unlike fairy tales—are believed or at least believable, and that—unlike myths—are set in the recent past and involve normal human beings rather than ancient gods or demigods." A number of the urban legends about murderers have a partial basis in fact. For example, the legend of a young woman who is babysitting in a house where a killer is hiding upstairs is based on the real-life murder of Janet Christman. The tale of a demented clown who lures children into a van and murders them was inspired by serial killer John Wayne Gacy, who dressed up like a clown for children's parties. Likewise, the urban legend of a homicidal maniac wearing a bunny costume also has a basis in fact.

A poster named "Timothy C. Forbes" is credited with disseminating online the standard version of the legend of the Bunnyman. The story begins in Clifton, Virginia. In 1904, the town's insane asylum was forced to close because of a petition signed by members of the community. One of the fifteen buses transporting inmates to their new home crashed. Ten of the inmates survived and dashed into the woods. All of the inmates were apprehended, with the exception of Marcus Wallster and Douglas J. Griffin. Over the next few days, locals found the skinned carcasses of rabbits dangling from the branches of trees near the Colchester Overpass. The rabbits appeared to have been chewed apart. A search party eventually discovered the body of Marcus Wallster. Attached to his foot was a note that read, "You'll never find me, no matter how hard you try! Signed, the Bunny Man." Douglas Griffin continued roaming the woods until one day when police tracked him to the railroad tracks above the overpass. As he was trying to make his escape, Griffin was struck and killed by an oncoming train. To this day, locals still find the bloody corpses of half-eaten rabbits hanging from trees surrounding the bridge at Halloween. They also say that the Bunnyman has been seen creeping through the one-lane bridge tunnel beneath the overpass. People driving through the tunnel have reported that the Bunnyman hurled an axe at their car while standing on top of the overpass. Anyone unfortunate—or foolish—enough to be caught by the Bunnyman at midnight is found hanging from the entrance of the tunnel the next morning. The credibility of this is diminished by the fact that neither the insane asylum nor Wallster and Griffin ever existed.

A second variant of the legend features a teenage boy who dons a bunny costume and embarks on a murderous rampage. After killing his entire family, he hanged himself from the entrance of the bridge. Locals believe that anyone venturing into the area late at night runs the risk of being disemboweled by the ghost of the Bunnyman.

As fantastic as the legend of the Bunnyman sounds, it could be based on two separate incidents that occurred one week apart in Burke, Virginia, in 1970. Around midnight on October 19, Robert Bennett and his fiancée were on their way to a relative's house when they decided to park on Guinea Road. Suddenly, a man dressed in white yelled at them about trespassing and proceeded to smash the windshield with a hatchet. Miraculously, the couple was able to drive off without suffering any serious injuries. Later that night, they found the hatchet on the floorboard of their car. The couple's description of their assailant differed on one important point. Bennett told the police that the white costume had bunny ears; however, his fiancée said the attacker was wearing a conical pointed hat, similar to the hood of a Ku Klux Klansman.

A figure resembling the Bunnyman made another appearance on October 26. A construction security guard named Paul Phillips sighted a man wearing a bunny costume standing on the porch of an unfinished house on Guinea Road. When Phillips asked the stranger what he was doing there, the man began ranting about trespassing and began chopping at a porch post with an axe. During the subsequent police investigation, over fifty people reported seeing the Bunnyman. Stories on the cases

Supposedly, the mad killer known as "The Bunnyman" used this hatchet to smash the passenger side window of a car parked on Guinea Road on October 19, 1970. *KeeferC.*

appeared in several major newspapers, including the *Washington Post*. Both cases were eventually closed.

Beginning in 2003, local police began controlling access to Bunnyman Bridge, the Colchester Overpass. Today, Bunnyman Bridge, as the overpass has come to be known, is still popular with high school and college students eager to have a personal encounter with the Bunnyman, despite the fact that it is illegal to loiter on public roads and to trespass on posted railroad tracks in Fairfax County, Virginia. The Bunnyman legend is also being kept alive by several movies, including *Donnie Darko* (2001) and three Bunnyman movies: *The Bunnyman Massacre* (2011), *Bunnyman 2* (2014) and *Bunnyman Vengeance* (2017).

THE HERRINGTON LAKE MONSTER

Mercer, Garrard and Boyle Counties, Kentucky

Located in Mercer, Garrard and Boyle Counties in Kentucky, Herrington Lake was created in 1925 with the construction of a dam on the Dix River to generate hydroelectric power. At the time, the Dix Dam was the largest manmade earthen structure in the world. The dam also serves as the site of the Kentucky Utilities main dispatch and communication center. The deepest lake in Kentucky contains a variety of gamefish, including largemouth bass, spotted bass, striped bass, white bass, blue, catfish and crappie. Some people believe that Herrington Lake is also home to a monster.

Sightings of a strange creature were reported not long after the lake's construction. Dubbed the "eel pig" because it has a pig-like snout and a slender, eel-shaped body, the twelve-to-fifteen-foot-monster is said to be able to swim as fast as a speedboat. The eel pig existed only in the tales told by sport fishermen until 1972, when Lawrence S. Thompson, a professor who owned a home on the lake, told a reporter for the *Louisville Courier* that he had seen the monster many times. He told that reporter that the beast was a monster "only in the sense that one would call an alligator a monster if they had never seen one before."

No other sighting of the Herrington Lake Monster has received the publicity that Professor Thompson's has. Nevertheless, eyewitnesses continue to tell their stories within the area. Over the years, several explanations for the creature's existence have been generated. The discovery of a pig's head in the lake by two dogs led the owners to believe that they had found evidence of the existence of the eel pig because the nearest slaughterhouse was miles away. Some locals believe that the prehistoric anomaly migrated down the Kentucky River from the Mississippi River as it followed its prey and became trapped in Herrington Lake after the dam was constructed. Others think that it swam through a series of limestone tunnels after the flooding of the Dix River. Biologists have suggested that the Herrington Lake Monster could actually be a previously undiscovered species of alligator. The most unpopular theory among people who claim to have seen the beast is that it is nothing more than a prank that has been perpetrated on a gullible public for decades.

CHASING "CHESSIE" ON THE CHESAPEAKE BAY

Hopewell, Virginia

A mysterious aquatic animal nicknamed "Chessie" has been seen swimming in the Chesapeake Bay since the 1880s. The website of the Maryland Department of Natural Resources describes it as a serpentine creature with a football-shaped head and a long, slender neck. It is between twenty and thirty feet in length. Some eyewitnesses claim that Chessie has side flippers and horns on its body. Most of the sightings have taken place on the eastern part of the Bay in early spring and summer.

The beast's best-known appearances began in the second half of the twentieth century. In 1963, a large, snake-like creature was spotted from a helicopter at Bush River. The first photographic evidence of Chessie's existence appeared in 1982, when a Maryland businessman named Robert Frew videotaped an undulating serpentine creature from his Kent Island home on Chesapeake Bay at 7:30 p.m. on Memorial Day. On August 20, 1982, the Enigma Project, under the direction of Mike Frizell, persuaded the Smithsonian Institute to examine the two-minute-long tape. The Smithsonian's researchers determined that the image was a "dark, elongated animate object" and not logs or marine animals. Because the Smithsonian report was inconclusive, the Enigma Project submitted the tape to the Applied Physics Laboratory at Johns Hopkins University for detailed computer enhancement. The lab also detected a snake-like form on the tape, but nothing more. The lab halted further enhancements of the tape due to the lack of funding. The videotape has not been subjected to further scientific scrutiny since 1983. That same year, Clyde Taylor and his daughter Carol reported seeing a thirty-foot-long serpentine creature in the bay, but they were unable to photograph it.

In 1988, a number of eyewitnesses saw what they described as a manatee in the James River near Richmond and in the Appomattox River near Hopewell. Another manatee that had traveled far from its home in Florida was spotted in the Chesapeake Bay around the same time. Scientists christened the beast "Chessie," implying that manatees had been misidentified as the elusive sea monster. As a result of the publicity the manatees received in the press, the number of sea monster sightings has dropped off dramatically, although a few reports are still filed every year. Some die-hard believers in Chessie (the sea monster) prefer to believe that it might have found a quieter home somewhere else.

DEVIL MONKEYS

The Southeast

In the 1960s, cryptozoologist Loren Coleman coined the term "Napes" for North American apes, a group of chimpanzee-like primates that skeptics say exist only in legend. These devil monkeys, as they have come to be known in the Midwest and the Southeast, are said to have bushy tails, tiny pointed ears, three toes, clawed feet and a brown-and-white patch on their underbellies. People also say they are able to jump up to twenty feet and to run at great speeds with their kangaroo-like legs. They stand between three or four feet in height, although some people claim to have seen a devil monkey that was seven feet tall. Encounters with these aggressive, shaggy simians have been reported throughout several southeastern states.

The first sighting of a devil monkey was reported in 1934 in South Pittsburgh, Tennessee. This eyewitness account, which was published in several national newspapers, described the beast as having the ability to "leap across fields" with "lightning speed." Some experts in the field of cryptozoology deduced that the "mystery kangaroos" that had been seen throughout the country for many years may have actually been devil monkeys.

The first "official" devil monkey attack took place in 1959. A Mr. and Mrs. Boyd were passing through the mountains near Saltville, Virginia, when their car was attacked by a mysterious creature. The Boyds' daughter told the authorities that the ape-like beast had taffy-colored hair, short front legs and well-developed back legs.

The next widely publicized encounter with a devil monkey occurred in 1960. Two Virginia nurses were driving home from work early in the morning when a baboon-like creature charged their car. It ripped the convertible top completely off while they escaped.

Nine years later, Barbara Mullins had an uncanny experience while driving through a rural area on Highway 12 in Louisiana. Suddenly, she spotted a bizarre-looking animal lying on the side of the road. She stopped her car and walked over to the carcass for a closer look. On close inspection, the animal appeared to be the size of a Saint Bernard dog, covered with thick, black hair. Its facial features resembled those of a baboon. It also had small, pointed ears and extended feet. Before leaving the site, Mullins took several photographs of the beast. Not surprisingly, her pictures created a sensation among biologists and cryptozoologists.

In 1979, a similar creature made an appearance in rural Georgia. Dubbed the "Belt Road Booger" in the local newspaper, the animal was described by a female eyewitness as having "a tail like a beaver's but it was bushy." She also described it as having a "dog-like face."

In 1996, a biologist for a biotechnology firm posted a report online about a sighting he had of the creature. He was gazing out at a field in the rain when he saw a strange animal running toward him on all fours from the adjacent property. Suddenly, it leaped over the five-foot fence in a single jump and landed about thirty feet away from him. "It had really big, yellowish eyes, large pointed ears, and a sparse coat of shaggy fur," he said. "It stood on its tiptoes and had a long, somewhat bushy tail, kind of like a squirrel, but not nearly as thickly furred." He ended his report by saying, "I know I saw something that day that I could not explain, and I am hard pressed to ask others to blindly accept what I say at face value."

A number of explanations have been presented to explain the origin of the strange monkey-like beings. The Choctaw tribe had a legend about a black, humanoid creature called the Nalusa Faly, which slid like a snake as it slithered up to its victims. Some researchers believe that these mysterious monkeys are descended from an extinct primate known as the *Theropithecus oswaldi*. Whatever these weird little beasts are, they seem to exist in a terrain far more real than the nightmares of people who have actually seen them.

THE LIZARD MAN OF SCAPE ORE SWAMP

Bishopville, South Carolina

Bishopville is a small rural town in the Pee Dee region of South Carolina, not far from larger cities like Florence, Sumter, Camden and Columbia. The town's website states that Bishopville is the home of the "Bishopville Opera House, the South Carolina Cotton Museum, the James House, Pearly Fryar's Topiary Garden, and many more attractions." Ironically, the website makes no mention of one of its most notorious attractions: the Lizard Man of Scape Ore Swamp.

The legend of the Lizard Man began in the early morning hours of June 29, 1988. Seventeen-year-old Christopher Davis was driving home from work when he had a flat tire right next to Scape Ore Swamp. He climbed out of his car and walked to the trunk to get his jack when suddenly, a green, lizard-like creature approximately seven feet tall began pounding on his car. As Davis struggled to drive away, he observed that the beast had scales, red eyes and long black claws. When he returned home, he discovered that the monster had gouged the roof of his car and ripped off the side mirror.

Two weeks later, local police received word of a car that had been vandalized much as Davis's vehicle had been. The investigating officers found long, deep scratches along the side of the car, just as if someone had used a very sharp instrument. They also found that someone—or something—had bent the antenna and ripped off the fenders. Even more baffling was the damage that had been done to the chrome trim. It appeared to have been chewed off by something with very large teeth. The police continued to receive reports of cars that had been attacked near Scape Ore Swamp for the next few weeks. They also made plaster casts of three-toed footprints that were found in the muddy ground. By early fall, though, the reports had ceased altogether.

Ever since the first sighting of the Lizard Man, tourism to Bishopville has skyrocketed. Not only has the legend of the Lizard Man been kept alive in countless T-shirts, but the artistic renderings of local artist Robert Howell have also been part of the official Lizard Man historical exhibit at Bishopville's South Carolina Cotton Museum. Interest in the local monster has risen so much in recent years that in June 2018, the first annual Lizard Man Festival and Comic Con was held at Bishopville. Interestingly enough, the Lizard Man might exist in places other than local folklore. In the summer of 2015, a woman leaving church one Sunday morning took a photograph of a large, lizard-like creature with her cellphone.

THE ROUGAROU

Houma, Louisiana

Shapeshifters—human beings who have the ability to transform themselves into animals—can be traced back thousands of years to the *Epic of Gilgamesh* and the myths of the ancient Greeks. For example, Zeus, the king of the gods, appeared before mortals in the guise of a variety of creatures, including a bull, an eagle, a swan, a cuckoo and a gopher. Shapeshifting can also be found in folklore all over the world, including England, Scotland, Ireland, Armenia, India, the Philippines, Japan, Korea, Trinidad and Chile. The best-known type of shapeshifting is lycanthropy, which involves the transformation of a human being into a wolf.

Tales of these creatures can be traced back to medieval France, when stories of the *loup garou*, or werewolf, were told to children to stay out of the woods, although many adults believed in them as well. By the sixteenth century, lycanthropy was thought to be a genetic disorder. The disease would remain dormant until it was triggered by some sort of traumatic experience. The victim would be covered with hair and would develop an intense hunger for meat. The transformation would be complete after the victim had had his or her first taste of human flesh.

When the werewolf tales were brought to Louisiana by French Canadians or by other French immigrants, the pronunciation of loup garou was changed to "rougarou." The Cajun version of the French werewolf developed its own distinctive characteristics over the years. It is said to have red eyes and sharp, canine-like teeth. Eyewitnesses describe it as standing between seven and eight feet tall. In most of the tales, the rougarou is a denizen of the Louisiana swampland, although a number of sightings have taken place in New Orleans. Wolf-like growls that are occasionally heard in New Orleans have been attributed to the elusive rougarou. People say that anyone—librarians, dentists, neighbors—can change into a rougarou in the light of the full moon. The metamorphosis can be voluntary, or it can be the result of a curse. Some Catholics claim that believers who do not observe the rules of Lent for seven consecutive years will be punished with the curse of lycanthropy. It has also been said that the curse is transferred to anyone who looks into the eyes of a rougarou. In another variant of the rougarou legend, people who are under a 101-day curse by a voodoo priestess or a witch can change into a werewolf. When the victim draws another person's blood, the curse is transferred. To guard against being attacked by a rougarou, some people place thirteen small objects, like coins, outside their front door. Because rougarous cannot count past twelve, their frustration level will mount, and they will continue trying to count the objects until sunrise, when they are forced to return to the darkness of their lairs.

Like many places that are unlucky—or lucky—enough to be closely linked to a strange creature, Louisiana has capitalized on the public's fascination with its local monster. Back when the New Orleans Pelicans basketball team was known as the Hornets, the owner considered changing its name to "The Rougarous." An exhibit dedicated to the rougarou can be found in the Audubon Zoo. The City of Houma holds a Rougarou Fest every year. To this day, a person who carouses late at night in Louisiana is referred to as someone who goes around "rougarouing." Clearly, the rougarou is resisting being confined to the annals of folklore.

THE TEXAS GOATSUCKER

Cuero, Texas

Phylis Canion is well acquainted with wild animals. While living in Africa, she shot and killed a zebra and a number of other beasts, the mounted heads of which now hang from the walls of her home on a ranch in Cuerro, Texas. Since moving to Cuerro, Texas, she has become acquainted with another creature far more exotic—and mysterious—than any that she had encountered. In 2005, she suspected that a bizarre predator was in the area when she inspected the cage containing two dozen of her newly hatched chicks and was shocked to find that something had pulled off their heads and drained their bodies of blood. Noting was left but bones. At that moment, Phylis recalled that six of her kittens had gone missing shortly before this incident. She asked her neighbors if they had noticed a strange animal on their ranches, and they told her that something had killed their goats. Like Phylis's chicks, the goats had been sucked dry. One of them told her that a vampire-like creature must have been responsible.

Phylis did not give much thought to her neighbor's seemingly outrageous theory until July 2007. She was driving on a road outside her ranch when she saw something strange along the side of the road. She pulled over and found what appeared to be a grayish-blue, hairless, dog-like animal that had been hit by a car. Her curiosity aroused, Phylis loaded the carcass into her car and took it home, where she put it in the freezer. "I've seen a lot of nasty stuff," Phylis told a reporter. "I've never seen anything like this. She and her neighbors discovered a total of three strange carcasses. By the end of the month, the forty-pound carcasses of three weird canines were found in the area.

Phylis's neighbors told her that the animals were not dogs or coyotes. They were chupacabras. The first report of a chupacabra surfaced in the east of Puerto Rico in 1995. Madelyne Tolention was gazing out her window when she saw what she described as an alien-like creature. As word of her sighting spread, so did the number of sightings. A number of people claimed that something had drained the blood out of the bodies of their goats. With the help of the internet, tales of the chupacabra spread throughout Latin America before reaching the United States. Benjamin Radford, a research fellow with the Committee for Skeptical Inquiry, determined through DNA analysis that the chupacabra carcasses discovered in Texas were actually the bodies of coyotes, dogs, foxes and raccoons. Radford believes that these animals have been misidentified as chupacabras because they have contracted sarcoptic mange, which is caused by itch-inducing mites. Once infested, the beasts lose their hair. Many of these diseased animals have black, thickened skin, as well as self-inflicted bite wounds.

THE FOUKE MONSTER

Fouke, Arkansas

In 1889, a Seventh-day Adventist minister named James M. Fouke established a colony along the Texarkana, Shreveport and Natchez Railroad. The town was named for lumberman and railroad executive James Fouke, who donated the land for the construction of a school in 1902. Today, Fouke is part of the Texarkana area at the intersection of Highway 71 and Interstate 49. According to the 2010 census, 859 people reside here. Chances are good that the census did not include Fouke's most famous resident.

Reports of a strange creature appear throughout the history of Fouke, Arkansas. The first recorded sighting of the bigfoot-like monster occurred in 1946, when a woman told Sheriff Leslie Greer that a hairy monster had been creeping around her home. The most famous sighting took place in May 1971, when a humanoid-like creature prowled around Bobby Ford's house for several days. His wife told him that she was asleep in the front room one evening when she saw a hairy arm reach through the window. As the terrified woman ran out of the room, she noticed that the monster had sharp claws and red eyes. Ford told a local constable that a few days later, Ford and several of his hunting buddies had returned from a hunt late in the evening when they spotted a huge figure standing in back of the house. They fired several shots at the beast, which appeared to fall to the ground. Ford, meanwhile, ran into the house when he heard his wife screaming. He was running through the house when a hairy seven-foot-tall creature grabbed him across the shoulder. Ford recalled that the monster had red eyes, that it breathed heavily and that its chest was about three feet wide. Somehow, Ford wrenched himself out of the creature's grasp and crashed through the front door. The others fired at the creature several times as it ran out of the house. The next day, the sheriff's department found no trace of the monster's blood on the property; however, investigators did find a strange set of tracks in the yard and the claw marks on the porch.

The Monster Mart in Fouke, Arkansas, recalls a terrifying night in May 1971 when a bigfoot-like creature terrorized Bobby Ford and his wife. *Reagscoop.*

A few weeks later, Bobby Ford told his story to Jim Powell, a reporter for the *Texarkana Gazette* and the *Texarkana Daily News*, and Dave Hall, director of Texarkana radio station KTFS, who drove out to the Fords' house to do a news story on the creature's attack. By the time the men arrived, the Ford family was in the middle of packing. They had decided to leave, even though they had owned the house for less than a week. After getting the story from Bobby Ford and his wife, Powell and Hall returned to the office and wrote it up. The next day, the follow-up story was published in the *Texarkana Gazette* and the *Texarkana Daily*. The reporters referred to the creature as the "Fouke Monster." When the story was picked up by the Associated Press and United Press International, the Fouke Monster became world-famous. Three years later, a low-budget documentary titled *The Legend of Boggy Creek* featured interviews with several eyewitnesses and residents of Fouke, Arkansas. It gained the Fouke Monster, as it has come to be known, an even larger audience.

THE LAKE WORTH MONSTER

Fort Worth, Texas

One hot day in July 1969, a crowd of people at Lake Worth, Texas, near Green Island saw an immense, humanoid creature standing on a cliff. They described it as standing over seven feet tall and weighing approximately 350 pounds. The next day, the local newspaper, the *Star-Telegram*, covered the incident in a front-page story titled "Fishy Man-Goat Terrifies Couples Parked at Lake Worth." According to the article, six people informed police that they had been attacked by a creature that was half-man and half-goat. They added that it was covered with fur and scales. One of the witnesses, John Reichart, claimed that the animal had jumped on the top of his car and left an eighteen-inch-long scratch on the side. Four units of Fort Worth police arrived at the area where the sightings had occurred, but they were unable to find any traces of the beast. They began to take the case more seriously when the next night, a dozen people watched the beast throw a tire at them from a bluff while making what one witness described as a "pitiful cry."

Before long, over one hundred hunters and trackers descended on Lake Worth. One of these visitors was Sallie Anne Clark, who wrote a book about the monster titled *Lake Worth Monster of Green Island, Fort Worth, Texas.* Over the course of her research, Clarke interviewed a number of the witnesses. Five of them told her that they saw the beast grab the thick limb of an oak tree and break it. Another witness, Jim Stephens, said he got a close look at the monster one night when it jumped on the hood of his Mustang, hanging on until the car crashed into the tree. Stephens observed that the creature was "human like" and covered with what appeared to be burn scars. After the book was self-published in September 1969, Clarke said that she saw the monster on three occasions.

Over the remainder of the summer, people reported seeing a seven-foot monster running through the Johnson grass. A number of them found tracks larger than human footprints. Dead sheep were reported to the police as well. The sightings abruptly ceased when school started. The furor over the "Goat Man" was reignited in November when Allen Plaster photographed a hairy beast wandering through the tall grass. Positive identification of the creature was impossible because the photograph was so grainy.

Not everyone in Fort Worth believed the monster was real, despite the number of people who claimed to have seen it. Many people believed that the creature was a hoax perpetrated by a local wearing a monster costume. The hoax theory received some confirmation in 2005 when a reporter for the *Fort Worth Star-Telegram* received a letter from someone claiming to be one of four high school students who decided to wear a tinfoil mask and scare people. Four years later, an unidentified man told a reporter for *Fort Worth, Texas* magazine that he had thrown a tire at a crowd of people from a bluff. Nevertheless, the Fort Worth Nature Center and Refuge holds a Lake Worth Monster Bash each October to commemorate that sultry summer in 1969 when a hairy, scaly monster roamed the Lake Worth area.

THE ST. AUGUSTINE MONSTER

St. Augustine, Florida

Anastasia Island was practically abandoned during a cool spell in November 30, 1896, when two boys, Herbert Coles and Dunham Coretter, discovered a strange-looking aquatic creature half-buried on the beach. At first, the boys believed they had found a whale. They immediately contacted Dr. De Witt Webb, the founder of the St. Augustine Historical

Society and Institute of Science, and asked him to inspect their find. When Dr. Webb arrived at the site, he agreed with the boys that the pinkish blob was a whale. Upon further inspection, however, Dr. Webb concluded that the beast was not a whale because of the stumps of what seemed to be tentacles.

Convinced that these were the remains of a giant octopus, Dr. Webb contacted Yale professor Addison E. Verrill for verification. Dr. Verrill studied Dr. Webb's report and agreed that this was indeed the carcass of a giant octopus. Dr. Verrill then gave a newspaper interview during which he announced the discovery of the creature, which he dubbed "Octopus gigantus verrill." However, after examining a sample of the carcass, Dr. Verrill decided that the "monster" was actually part of a sperm whale's head. His revised opinion of the "thing's" identity did not receive nearly the same amount of press coverage as his original conclusion had.

Meanwhile, Dr. Webb sent his tissue samples and a number of photographs to the Smithsonian Institute, including his measurements of the beast: "The body measures 18 feet in length by 10 feet in breadth.... It must weigh not less than 5 or 6 tons and is, of course, quite offensive." As time passed, most of Dr. Webb's photographs were misplaced, and the story of the St. Augustine Monster was relegated to the status of an obscure historical footnote. By the 1970s, however, the Smithsonian began receiving requests for tissue samples of the monster. In 1971, comparative tests with mammal tissue proved that the beast was a giant octopus. This conclusion was supported in 1986 by tests for amino acids. In 2004, though, DNA tests identified the sample as whale blubber.

THE SKUNK APE

Ochopee, Florida

The skunk ape, also known as the "swamp ape," "swamp cabbage man" and "Swampsquatch," is a bigfoot-like creature that has been sighted in North Carolina and Arkansas but has been seen primarily in Florida. Its name is derived from its foul, skunk-like stench. Sightings of the hairy, bipedal monster peaked in the 1960s and the 1970s. A number of highly publicized personal encounters with the skunk ape were reported in the suburban neighborhoods of Dade County.

Dave Sheahy, the director of the Skunk Ape Research Headquarters in Ochopee, Florida, is one of the state's foremost authorities on the beast. Sheahy's lifelong fascination with the creature stems from an encounter he had in 1974 when he was ten years old. He and his brother saw the ape when they were deer hunting in what is now the Big Cypress National Preserve. "It was walking across the swamp, and my brother spotted it first," Sheahy said. "It looked like a man, but completely covered with hair." As rain began falling from the sky, the monster ran off into the cypress hammocks.

Since then, Sheahy has made numerous television appearances and written a field guide. He has also conducted many investigations of reports that filter into the Research Headquarters. He estimates that seven to nine skunk apes are inhabiting the Everglades. Sheahy describes the average male skunk ape as standing six to seven feet tall and weighing approximately 450 pounds. The average female skunk ape stands five to six feet tall and weighs 250 pounds. Their long red or black hair is similar to that of a gorilla or orangutan. Most eyewitnesses run into skunk apes accidentally, but Sheahy has sighted three of them in his "hunts." He captured one of his encounters on video in 2000. In the 1:38-minute footage, the creature seems to be strolling through a hammock of palm trees before breaking into a run.

So far, no sightings of the skunk ape have been verified by the National Park Service wildlife staff. Skeptics like Joe Nickell believe that most of these creatures are misidentified black bears. Sheahy answers those critics who ask why no remains of the beast have been found by saying that carcasses decay very quickly in the swamp. Most people agree that the skunk ape will remain a legendary creature until definitive proof of its existence (i.e., an actual skunk ape) is found.

THE GRUNCH

New Orleans, Louisiana

The Grunch is a legendary monster that is reputed to have killed pets and farm animals in Puerto Rico and in different parts of the United States. New Orleans has its own version of the "goat sucker." The legendary beast is closely connected to the legend of Marie Laveau. After the birth of a deformed infant known as the Devil Baby, Laveau tried to prevent the creature from reproducing by castrating it. The testicles fell to the floor in a puddle of blood and instantly transformed into a male and female Grunch. The demonic pair pounced on the Voodoo Queen, biting her multiple times. The elderly woman passed out from the intense pain. When she regained consciousness, the creatures were gone.

This distinctive breed of chupacabra is said to stand three to four feet tall. This goat-like creature has gray scaly skin and spiny projections along its back. The monster's howl has been likened to the cry of a banshee. People say it drains the blood of its prey through a single hole. Its approach is marked by an overwhelming odor.

An entirely different origin story is set in an old road in the eastern part of New Orleans that came to be known as Grunch Road. This isolated area was said to be inhabited by a small colony of social outcasts, mostly albinos and dwarves. Over time, they inbred and produced a mutant creature the locals referred to as "the Grunch." The beasts were ravenous creatures who were blamed for the disappearances of farm animals and human beings. In a more supernatural version of the legend, members of the group sold their souls to Satan in exchange for his protection. Their pact with the devil involved the sacrifice of small animals. The Grunch uses its ability to mimic the cry of an injured goat to lure passersby on Grunch Road to their door.

15

LOST TREASURE TALES

THE LOST CONFEDERATE TREASURY

Wilkes County, Georgia

On April 2, 1865, Confederate president Jefferson Davis was leaving church when he received word that Richmond, the capital of the Confederacy, was in imminent danger of being captured by Union forces because Lee's defensive line had been penetrated. Davis then informed his cabinet that the evacuation of Richmond was underway. To prevent the treasury from falling into the hands of the Yankees, Davis said that they would have to take the gold with them. The plan was to load the cabinet members, valuables and gold onto two trains no later than 8:00 p.m. The cabinet members would ride on the first train, and the "special cargo," consisting of gold ingots, silver bricks and gold and silver coins, would be loaded onto the second train under the command of navy captain William H. Parker. In desperation, young midshipmen from a training ship on the James Rivers were used as the military guard. Several of them were as young as twelve years old.

Loading the trains took so long that the trains were unable to leave Richmond until after midnight. The trains rumbled through the night until reaching Danville, where the tracks ended. Davis and his cabinet continued their exodus from Richmond on horseback; the "special cargo" was transferred to wagons in containers that had once contained sugar,

Just before the fall of Richmond, Virginia, in May 1865, Confederate president Jefferson Davis authorized the transport of the Confederate treasury on two trains. *Library of Congress, Prints & Photographs Division, AL-424.*

ammunition, coffee and flour. Concern that the cavalry might be in the area led Captain Parker to take evasive action, zig-zagging across the South Carolina–Georgia state line. After a while, control of the second train was passed to Secretary of War John C. Breckenridge, who, in turn, put Brigadier General Basil Duke in charge. Duke had the gold and valuables moved to six wagons. The escorts were Duke's own soldiers and the midshipmen. Eight of Duke's men rode on each of the six wagons.

After passing through Greensboro in the direction of the Oconee River, the wagons split up to confuse the Yankees hot on their trail. Davis held his last cabinet meeting on May 10, 1865, in Washington, Georgia. In his last official act as president, Davis appointed Micajah Clark the acting treasurer of the Confederacy. Not long afterward, Davis and his staff were captured by Union forces, along with the bulk of the treasure. Meanwhile, Brigadier General Duke paid each of the one thousand men in his command $26.25 from his treasure wagons near Irwinville. Then Duke and his men headed toward Washington. On May 24, 1865, Duke and his soldiers were camping at the Chennault Plantation in Lincoln County when they were attacked by bandits, who made off with $251,029 from the cache. Approximately $111,000 was recovered by bank officials.

Stories of buried treasure abound in Wilkes County. For years, residents told the tale of the bushwhackers' shuffling through piles of god and silver coins as they dumped handfuls of gold into sacks. People said that the bags were so overloaded that the bandits were forced to hide hundreds of the coins as they rode through Wilkes County. According to another legend, the soldiers buried much of the treasure along the banks of the Oconee River near Parker's Ferry, burned the wagons and rode off. Others say that gold coins were found near Chennault Plantation. The most fascinating legend generated by the missing gold appeared in a book written by a former schoolteacher titled *Snow White Sands*. In her book, Martha Mizell Puckett claimed that during his final cabinet meeting, Davis divided the Confederate treasury among his staff. In a variant of the legend, a Confederate sympathizer named Sylvester Mumford was given the entire treasury for safekeeping. Mumford placed some of the gold on a British steamer headed for England. His daughter, Goertner "Gertrude" Mumford, ended up with the rest of the treasury. When she died at the age of ninety-nine in 1946, her will established the Sylvester Mumford Memorial Endowment at the Thornwell Orphanage in Clinton, South Carolina. Her will also established two scholarship funds. In his article "The Search for Lost Confederate Gold," Hans Kuenzi concluded that only $70,000 of the gold from the Confederate treasury is missing.

THE TREASURE OF HAMPTON PLANTATION

Charleston, South Carolina

In 1701, Daniel McGregor issued a warrant for five hundred acres of land that had been previously occupied by the Sewee Indians. The next year, Jacob LaPonte and Elias Horry purchased the land from McGregor. Over the next twenty-six years, a number of different people owned the plantation. Then in 1735, Anthony Bonneau sold the land to Noe Serre, who immediately began constructing a mansion on the property. In 1757, he bequeathed the plantation and his slaves to Daniel Huger Horry. He added two wings to the house in the 1760s. During the Revolutionary War, the British searched Hampton Plantation twice, even though Horry was a Loyalist. After the war, Horry set about restoring his plantation. Following Daniel Horry's death in 1785, his wife, Harriott, and her mother, Eliza Lucas Pinckey, built a portico on the side of the house. Their most famous visitor was George Washington. In 1797, Harriott's daughter moved into Hampton Plantation with her new husband, Frederick Rutledge. By the time Frederick died in 1824, he and Harriott had had eight children. In 1830, Harriott Horry Rutledge inherited

In 1937, Archibald Rutledge discovered a small box under a section of old wallpaper detailing the location of his grandfather's treasure chest at Hampton Plantation. The chest has never been found. *Brian Stansberry*.

the estate after her mother, Harriott, died. The next owner was Henry Middleton Rutledge, the grandson of Harriott Horry Rutledge. After his first wife, Anna, died in 1876, Henry Middleton Rutledge married Margaret Hamilton Seabrook. Their son, Archibald Rutledge, became a schoolteacher in Pennsylvania and the first poet laureate of South Carolina. He returned to Hampton Plantation in 1937. That same year, he wrote a book about the estate. The South Carolina State Park service acquired the property in 1971 following Rutledge's death.

One of the most frequently told stories about Hampton Plantations concerns a discovery made by Archibald Rutledge in 1937 as he was restoring the house. He was working in his garden when he dug up several Spanish silver coins, brass work, thirty-six Delft tiles and two thousand antique bottles. His discoveries did not end there. While Rutledge was working inside the house, he removed a section of old wallpaper. Underneath, Rutledge found a small box. Inside was a folded map on which was drawn a cross and what appeared to be a treasure chest. Over the next two years, he found a crock of coins in the yard, but the treasure chest eluded him. In his book about Hampton Plantation, Rutledge speculated about his grandfather's attempts to conceal the family fortune during the Civil War. So far, the treasure chest has never been found.

THE LOST MINE OF PERCY SHULTS

Gatlinburg, Tennessee

Gatlinburg, Tennessee, is a popular resort town bordering the Great Smoky Mountains National Park. Long before tourists began flocking to the scenic mountain town to "get away from it all" in its picturesque cabins, the area was home to the Cherokee Indians, who accessed their hunting grounds using the Indian Gap Trail. The abundance of game attracted fur traders, who camped in present-day Gatlinburg. In the early nineteenth century, settlers entered the region using the old Indian Gap Trail. One of the first white men to set up permanent residence here was William Ogle, who built a cabin in the mountains in 1806. Many of these settlers had received land grants for serving in the American Revolution and the War of 1812. The town derived its name from Radford Gatlin, who moved there in 1854. In 1857, Gatlin established a post office in his general store. Gatlin was driven out in 1859 because he was a Confederate sympathizer living in a town populated by people with largely antislavery sentiments. Following the Civil War, the logging industry brought prosperity to the area. The character of the town began to change even more in the early 1900s when tourists started trickling in to partake of the natural beauty of the Smoky Mountains. Today, the past peacefully coexists with the present in Gatlinburg. One of the town's oldest legends, which is still told around campfires today, dates to the town's beginnings.

In the mid-1800s, one of the descendants of Gatlinburg's earliest settlers, Percy Shults, made his living as a blacksmith at Pittman Center. In 1867, Shults decided to supplement his income by acquiring a ninety-nine-year lease on the mineral rights around the headwaters of Porter Creek. Shult's neighbors noticed that every year, he and his wife left their home and made their way to their mine, using a different route each time to avoid detection. While Shults worked in the mine around the Pinnacle of Greenbrier, his wife sat patiently waiting for him on a rock. As the legend grew, so did the size of his mine; by the early twentieth century, people were estimating that Shults's mine extended all the way to North Carolina. People of a more realistic bent believed that Shults discovered only a small gold streak in his mine.

Over time, Shults's wealth increased considerably. It was rumored by some that he had found a cache of coins from the Civil War era around his claim. His skill as a blacksmith led some of his neighbors to conclude that Shults had received stolen treasury plates from a friend and was minting his own silver coins. When the Secret Service learned that the coins Shults and his wife had been spending had an unusually high silver content, agents traveled to the Smoky Mountains to investigate. Shults and his wife received news that the agents were coming and headed west, never to be heard from again.

In the absence of hard facts, Shults's mine has entered the realm of folklore. The directions to his lost mine seem to vary from one decade to the next. The legend of the Shults mine was revived in the 1960s after the new owners of Shults's home in Pittman Center found a clay pot containing silver and gold coins dating to the nineteenth century.

THE STRANGE SAGA OF THE BEALE CIPHERS

Lynchburg, Virginia

The legend of the Beale Ciphers begins in 1817, when a man named Thomas J. Beale led a band of thirty adventurers from Virginia to the Spanish province of Santa Fe de Nuevo Mexico to hunt buffalo. They had been following one particular herd for two weeks when they decided to encamp in a small ravine about three hundred miles north. One of the hunters was exploring a cleft rock when he found what appeared to be flecks of gold. Before long, Beale's band had given up buffalo hunting and were devoting themselves full time to digging for gold. Many historians believe that they did most of their prospecting in present-day Colorado. After mining for eighteen months, the men assigned Beale the task of transporting the hoard of precious metals back to Virginia. He was told to bury the treasure in a secure location known only to him. Some people believe that Beale secreted away the treasure somewhere in Montvale in Bedford County, Virginia. He made several trips to the hidden location before creating three encrypted messages or cipher texts that revealed the location, a description of the treasure and the names of the miners and their relatives. The three cipher texts have come to be known as the Beale ciphers or Beale codes.

In 1822, Beale gave an iron box containing the cipher texts to a Lynchburg innkeeper named Robert Morris for safekeeping. Morris was told not to open the box for ten years unless Beale or a member of his party showed up earlier. A few months later, Morris received a letter from Beale promising him that an entrusted friend in St. Louis would mail him a key to the cipher texts. However, Beale's friend never sent the key, and Beale never traveled to Lynchburg to pick up the iron box. Fully expecting Beale to show up some time, the innkeeper did not open the iron box until 1845. It contained several pages of cryptotext and two letters from Beale.

In 1862, Morris gave the contents of the iron box to a friend, who is thought by many to be James B. Ward. He was able to decode the second cipher using the Declaration of Independence as a key. Ward numbered the words of the Declaration of Independence and substituted the first letter of each word for the corresponding number in Beale Cipher No. 2. To his chagrin, Ward discovered that the key to Beale Cipher No. 2 was not the key to Beale Ciphers No. 1 or No. 3. In 1885, Ward published the story of the Beale treasure in a twenty-three-page pamphlet titled *The Beale Papers*.

115, 73, 24, 807, 37, 52, 49, 17, 31, 62, 647, 22, 7, 15, 140, 47, 29, 107, 79, 84, 56,
239, 10, 26, 811, 5, 196, 308, 85, 52, 160, 136, 59, 211, 36, 9, 46, 316, 554, 122,
106, 95, 53, 58, 2, 42, 7, 35, 122, 53, 31, 82, 77, 250, 196, 56, 96, 118, 71, 140,
287, 28, 353, 37, 1005, 65, 147, 807, 24, 3, 8, 12, 47, 43, 59, 807, 45, 316, 101, 41,
78, 154, 1005, 122, 138, 191, 16, 77, 49, 102, 57, 72, 34, 73, 85, 35, 371, 59, 196,
81, 92, 191, 106, 273, 60, 394, 620, 270, 220, 106, 388, 287, 63, 3, 191, 122, 43,
234, 400, 106, 290, 314, 47, 48, 81, 96, 26, 115, 92, 158, 191, 110, 77, 85, 197, 46,
10, 113, 140, 353, 48, 120, 106, 2, 607, 61, 420, 811, 29, 125, 14, 20, 37, 105, 28,
248, 16, 159, 7, 35, 19, 301, 125, 110, 486, 287, 98, 117, 511, 62, 51, 220, 37, 113,
140, 807, 138, 540, 8, 44, 287, 388, 117, 18, 79, 344, 34, 20, 59, 511, 548, 107,
603, 220, 7, 66, 154, 41, 20, 50, 6, 575, 122, 154, 248, 110, 61, 52, 33, 30, 5, 38, 8,
14, 84, 57, 540, 217, 115, 71, 29, 84, 63, 43, 131, 29, 138, 47, 73, 239, 540, 52, 53,
79, 118, 51, 44, 63, 196, 12, 239, 112, 3, 49, 79, 353, 105, 56, 371, 557, 211, 515,
125, 360, 133, 143, 101, 15, 284, 540, 252, 14, 205, 140, 344, 26, 811, 138, 115,
48, 73, 34, 205, 316, 607, 63, 220, 7, 52, 150, 44, 52, 16, 40, 37, 158, 807, 37, 121,
12, 95, 10, 15, 35, 12, 131, 62, 115, 102, 807, 49, 53, 135, 138, 30, 31, 62, 67, 41,
85, 63, 10, 106, 807, 138, 8, 113, 20, 32, 33, 37, 353, 287, 140, 47, 85, 50, 37, 49,
47, 64, 6, 7, 71, 33, 4, 43, 47, 63, 1, 27, 600, 208, 230, 15, 191, 246, 85, 94, 511, 2
270, 20, 39, 7, 33, 44, 22, 40, 7, 10, 3, 811, 106, 44, 486, 230, 353, 211, 200, 31,
10, 38, 140, 297, 61, 603, 320, 302, 666, 287, 2, 44, 33, 32, 511, 548, 10, 6, 250,
557, 246, 53, 37, 52, 83, 47, 320, 38, 33, 807, 7, 44, 30, 31, 250, 10, 15, 35, 106,
160, 113, 31, 102, 406, 230, 540, 320, 29, 66, 33, 101, 807, 138, 301, 316, 353,
320, 220, 37, 52, 28, 540, 320, 33, 8, 48, 107, 50, 811, 7, 2, 113, 73, 16, 125, 11,
110, 67, 102, 807, 33, 59, 81, 158, 38, 43, 581, 138, 19, 85, 400, 38, 43, 77, 14, 27,
8, 47, 138, 63, 140, 44, 35, 22, 177, 106, 250, 314, 217, 2, 10, 7, 1005, 4, 20, 25,
44, 48, 7, 26, 46, 110, 230, 807, 191, 34, 112, 147, 44, 110, 121, 125, 96, 41, 51,
50, 140, 56, 47, 152, 540, 63, 807, 28, 42, 250, 138, 582, 98, 643, 32, 107, 140,
112, 26, 85, 138, 540, 53, 20, 125, 371, 38, 36, 10, 52, 118, 136, 102, 420, 150,
112, 71, 14, 20, 7, 24, 18, 12, 807, 37, 67, 110, 62, 33, 21, 95, 220, 511, 102, 811,
30, 83, 84, 305, 620, 15, 2, 108, 220, 106, 353, 105, 106, 60, 275, 72, 8, 50, 205,
185, 112, 125, 540, 65, 106, 807, 188, 96, 110, 16, 73, 33, 807, 150, 409, 400, 50,
154, 285, 96, 106, 316, 270, 205, 101, 811, 400, 8, 44, 37, 52, 40, 241, 34, 205,
38, 16, 46, 47, 85, 24, 44, 15, 64, 73, 138, 807, 85, 78, 110, 33, 420, 505, 53, 37,
38, 22, 31, 10, 110, 106, 101, 140, 15, 38, 3, 5, 44, 7, 98, 287, 135, 150, 96, 33, 84,
125, 807, 191, 96, 511, 118, 440, 370, 643, 466, 106, 41, 107, 603, 220, 275, 30,
150, 105, 49, 53, 287, 250, 208, 134, 7, 53, 12, 47, 85, 63, 138, 110, 21, 112, 140,
485, 486, 505, 14, 73, 84, 575, 1005, 150, 200, 16, 42, 5, 4, 25, 42, 8, 16, 811,
125, 160, 32, 205, 603, 807, 81, 96, 405, 41, 600, 136, 14, 20, 28, 26, 353, 302,
246, 8, 131, 160, 140, 84, 440, 42, 16, 811, 40, 67, 101, 102, 194, 138, 205, 51,
63, 241, 540, 122, 8, 10, 63, 140, 47, 48, 140, 288.

Anyone who can break the code for Thomas J. Beale's three cipher texts will discover the location of his buried gold. *Historicair.*

Because no one has been able to break the codes for Ciphers No. 1 and No. 3, the mystery of the Beale treasure has deepened over the years. Some of the more cynical residents of Lynchburg believe that the treasure has already been discovered. Others believe that the entire story is an elaborate hoax concocted by Beale, Morris, Ward or someone else. Hard-core treasure hunters still hold out hope that someday, a crucial piece of information will turn up and it will reveal the hidden location of the Beale treasure.

JAMES COPELAND'S GOLD

Hancock County, Mississippi

Born in Jackson County, Mississippi, on January 18, 1823, James Copeland's criminal career began when he stole a pocket knife from a neighbor at age twelve. In his early teens, he was indicted for the theft of several pigs from the same neighbor. A scoundrel from Mobile named Gale H. Wages persuaded Copeland's family to burn down the Jackson County Courthouse to save the boy from the gallows. Wages inducted Copeland into his gang, or "clan," which committed an assortment of crimes from the 1830s through the 1850s in Alabama, Mississippi and Louisiana, including murder, arson, the theft of slaves and the hijacking of flatboats. Copeland's life as a "land pirate" came to an abrupt end on October 30, 1857, when he was hanged on the banks of the Leaf River. He was buried near the Leaf River, but his corpse was exhumed three days later. Months later, his skeleton was displayed at McInnis and Dozier Drugstore in Hattiesburg before disappearing in the early 1900s.

Throughout the second half of the nineteenth century, people in Mississippi told tales of Copeland's buried gold. Shortly before Copeland's execution, he claimed to have buried $30,000 in a swamp near Mobile before re-burying it in Hancock County, somewhere near Pearlington in the Catahoula Swamp. Gold seekers in the 1960s concentrated their search in Gautier and Pascagoula, Mississippi. In the 1980s, the rumor spread of the discovery of a whiskey barrel containing $22,000 in gold coins in a Pascagoula swamp. Because of the distance between Pearlington and Pascagoula, some treasure hunters believe that this was not one of the three barrels containing $30,000.

In the 1990s and early 2000s, fortune hunters continued combing Mississippi's Gulf Coast for Copeland's buried loot. However, John D. W. Guice, who wrote the introduction to the 2008 edition of *The Life and Confessions of the Noted Outlaw James Copeland* by J.R.S. Pitts, believes that the rumors of Copeland's hidden gold are probably just rumors. He argues that if the Copeland Gang buried any gold at all, it would have probably been a small amount. After all, if the gang had amassed a small fortune, they would have had no reason to resort to counterfeiting.

16

UNDERGROUND MYSTERIES

THE MYSTERIOUS ORIGIN OF THE ALABAMA STONE

Tuscaloosa, Alabama

In 1817, Thomas Scales and his father moved from North Alabama to Tuscaloosa Falls. A few weeks later, they were clearing a plot of land on the west bank of Big Creek near Tuscaloosa when they made an amazing discovery. They had worked their way over to a four-foot-high embankment running from the creek to the river and found a half-buried teardrop-shaped piece of sandstone standing at the foot of a large poplar tree. On close examination, they found a Latin inscription carved on the face of the stone: *HISPAN ET IND REX 1232*, translated as *The King of Spain and the Indies*. Thomas and his father carried their find up to Tuscaloosa Falls. It ended up in the log cabin office of Leven Powell, Tuscaloosa County's first tax collector. For years, he kept it near the door. Then in 1824, Silas Dinsmore, a Mobile merchant, acquired the stone and sent it to the American Antiquarian Society in Worcester, Massachusetts, where it was catalogued as "The Alabama Stone." In 1963, seventeen-year-old Donald Guyver campaigned successfully for the return of the Alabama Stone to the state where it was found in 1817. The National Guard brought the Alabama Stone back to Tuscaloosa in October 1963. A week later, it was delivered to the Alabama Archives and History in

Montgomery. The strange rock was eventually placed in storage because it defied classification. It remains in storage to this day.

The ferruginous sandstone measures twenty-one and a half inches in length, eighteen inches in width and twelve inches in breadth. It weighs two hundred pounds. The surface of the stone is pock-marked with conical holes and "gash-shaped" cuts. Archaeologists have theorized that Native Americans used the conical holes as holders for chert rock cobbles as they were flaked, nuts as they were cracked or seeds as they were ground

The Alabama Stone was displayed in Boston as early evidence of European exploration in the New World. Indeed, Europeans frequently staked their land claims by carving letters and symbols on stones. After conquering Mexico and Peru, the Spanish established a mint in Mexico City in 1536, producing coins with wording similar to that which appears on the Alabama Stone. In their article "The Alabama Stone: A Warrior River Mystery," authors Caleb Curren and Steve Newby suggest that the date 1232 could have been a stone carver's error. They also offer three other explanations for the inscription on the Alabama Stone: (1) Tom Scales or his father perpetrated a hoax; (2) Native Americans made the inscription in the seventeenth, eighteenth or nineteenth centuries; (3) Europeans living in this part of Alabama in the sixteenth, seventeenth or eighteenth centuries made the inscription, possibly a land-claiming expedition after the Spanish reoccupied Pensacola Bay in 1723. As tantalizing as all these theories may be, the fact remains that we may never know the real story behind the Alabama Stone.

THE CHURCH HILL TUNNEL

Richmond, Virginia

In 1873, the Chesapeake and Ohio Railway (C&O) completed construction of a tunnel that would enable it to extend its line from a terminal in downtown Richmond to the new Peninsula Subdivision seventy-five miles southeast. Once the tracks were completed, coal could be transported to the new coal pier on the harbor of Hampton Roads. The railroad tracks entered the tunnel east of North Eighteenth Street and north of East Marshall Street. The east end of the tunnel opened up near Thirty-First Street. The construction of the tunnel was plagued with problems from the outset. Because the four-thousand-foot-long tunnel was dug through the blue marl clay shrink-swell, groundwater seepage was a serious problem. Before the tunnel was finished, ten workers were killed in several cave-ins.

The Church Hill Tunnel was abandoned in 1901 following the completion of the riverfront viaduct. Then in 1925, the railroad attempted to make enough repairs that the tunnel would be usable again. On October 2, 1925, the unthinkable happened. While dozens of workers were trying to shore up the tunnel, 190 feet of the ceiling near the western end collapsed, just as the steam engine locomotive 231 entered the tunnel, pulling ten flat cars. Two men—Richard Mosby and H. Smith—were probably buried alive. Their bodies were never found. Rescuers were able to recover the body of Joseph Mason, the engineer. The badly burned fireman, Benjamin F. Mosby, escaped out the eastern end of the tunnel, but he died a few hours later. Rescue efforts continued over the next week but were eventually halted as the result of further cave-ins. A few months later, the Virginia State Corporation Commission ordered the tunnel closed, sealing the locomotive, its ten flat cars and the bodies of two of the workers inside.

In the decades following the 1925 tragedy, the Church Hill Tunnel collapsed several other times. In 1962, a house was engulfed in another collapse and a worker was killed. To this day, evidence of the cave-ins can be seen in the dips in the north–south streets crisscrossing the tunnel. Although the railroad plugged up the western end of the tunnel, the eastern end was used as a turnaround for a connection with the Southern Railway's line. Vines and bushes covered the western end until the early 2000s when developers cleared the vegetation while remodeling the warehouses nearby. In 2006, the Virginia Historical Society announced its plans to recover the bodies of the buried men and the locomotive. Intrigued by the possibility of finding and preserving the historic locomotive, the History Channel expressed interest in assisting the Virginia Historical Society. However, when a hole was drilled and a camera was lowered into the tunnel, investigators discovered that water and silt had filled the tunnel. The project was put on hold over concern that excavations would cause the tunnel to collapse even more and create sinkholes that would destroy area homes. Today, the tunnel is surrounded by condominiums that have grown up around it.

The mystery of the tunnel's hidden secrets has given rise to a number of ghost legends. Curiosity seekers have been scared off by voices screaming, "Get me out!" Other ghostly noises include the sound of someone digging into the rubble and the grinding of the wheels of the locomotive on the steel rails. The most horrific tale concerns the sudden appearance of the "Richmond vampire." The creature has been described by eyewitnesses

On October 2, 1925, the Church Hill Tunnel collapsed, burying Locomotive 231, its ten flat cars and two members of its crew. *Ikmscott.*

as a blood-covered beast with sharp teeth. Folds of skin hang from its muscular frame. Shortly after the 1925 cave-in, rescue workers sighted the monster crawling its way out of the rock and debris and racing toward the James River. Several of the workers chased it into Hollywood Cemetery, where it ran into a mausoleum and vanished. Locals will undoubtedly continue to tell stories such as these until researchers find a way to bring the tunnel's contents to light.

THE DEVIL'S MILLHOPPER

Gainesville, Florida

Devil's Millhopper Geological State Park is located at Gainesville, Florida, off County Road 232. The park's main attraction is an enormous sinkhole 120 feet deep and 500 feet wide. It acquired its name from its resemblance to the funnel-shaped hopper of a grain mill. Twelve springs feed into the muddy pool at the bottom of the limestone hole. Because of the canopy of shaded trees surrounding the rim of the hole, the temperature on the inside remains dramatically cooler than the outside temperatures. The sinkhole was formed over the course of the past ten to fifteen thousand years when rain water combined with dead plant material created a weak acid that dissolved large deposits of limestone.

Curiosity seekers have been visiting the Devil's Millhopper since the 1880s. It was purchased by the State of Florida in 1974. The Devil's Millhopper is the only geological location in Florida's entire park system. Visitors to the park can walk down a wooden stairway of 232 steps to a viewer's platform at the bottom. They can learn about the natural history of the area through interpretive displays, such as collections of marine shells, sharks' teeth and the fossilized remains of extinct animals. The boardwalk and steps were damaged by Hurricane Irma in September 2017 and were closed down temporarily.

A number of different legends have contributed to the geological wonder's somewhat sinister overtones. The large number of fossilized bones of modern and prehistoric mammals that have been found inside the hole has led some to believe that the beasts were climbing down to meet the devil when they became trapped and drowned in the pond. The earliest legend is of Native American origin. The story goes that the devil lusted after an Indian princess and swallowed her up in the ground. In his book *Strange Florida: The Unexplained and Unusual*, author Charlie Carlson traces one local legend back to the early 1800s. A family was transporting a load of cotton in a mule-driven wagon when they heard a rumble from deep under the ground. Suddenly, a huge hole opened up in the earth, swallowing up trees, rocks, animals and at least one "likkered-up" sinner. Even today, tales are told of passersby who fell into the hole and are never heard from again.

THE TEXAS KILLING FIELDS

South Texas

The Killing Fields is located in a desolate fifty-mile area between Houston and Galveston on Interstate 45. Over thirty girls or young women have either disappeared or been found murdered in the Killing Fields since the body of fourteen-year-old Brenda Jones was discovered here on July 2, 1971. Many of the victims ranged in age from ten to twenty-four years. This remote area has been described by authorities as the ideal place for a serial killer to get rid of his victims. In a CBS interview, *Texas Monthly* reporter Skip Hollandsworth said, "It's a kind of environment that's sultry and sinister, easy to get to. You jump off of I-45. You drive down one of the dirt rutted roads. You dump the body. And you're gone for good." Ironically, the refineries of League City and Interstate 45 are in clear view of the Killing Fields.

The first of the Killing Fields murder victims was thirteen-year-old Colette Wilson. In June 17, 1971, she vanished after getting off at a bus stop after school. No trace of her was found until five months later when her corpse was discovered in the Killing Fields. She had been killed by a gunshot wound to the head. More murders of adolescent and teenage girls continued throughout the remainder of the decade. Convinced that a serial killer was responsible for the senseless murders, local police interviewed a number of suspects but were unable to connect them to any of the murders. The mystery of the Killing Fields intensified as the files of unsolved cases grew in the 1980s and 1990s. Not only were bodies found in the Killing Fields, but so were abandoned cars. After the mutilated body of sixteen-year-old Teresa Vanegas was found on November 3, 2006, the murders abruptly stopped.

Only a handful of the Killing Fields cases have been closed. One of these "cold cases" was the murder of Krystal Baker, the thirteen-year-old great-niece of Norma Jean Baker, otherwise known as actress Marilyn Monroe. On March 5, 1996, she ran out of her grandmother's house following a heated argument and made her way to a convenience store, where she called home. Her mother told her to return to her grandmother's house. Krystal left the convenience store and disappeared. Two hours later, her corpse was found near the I-10 Trinity River Bridge. She had been raped and strangled. Her murder remained unsolved until 2012, when a DNA test was performed on Kevin Edison Smith, who had been arrested for an unrelated crime in 2010. The test matched DNA taken from Krystal's underwear and dress. The jury deliberated for thirty minutes before convicting Edison of the murder of Krystal Baker. He was given life in prison without parole. So far, Smith has not been connected to any of the other Killing Field murders.

The sensationalistic murders at the Killing Fields captured the imagination of the public in the twenty-first century. In 2011, a movie titled *Texas Killing Fields* was made, starring Sam Worthington and Jeffrey Dean Morgan. In 2012, the CBS news show *48 Hours* filmed an episode on the Killing Fields. Until all of the murders are solved, more movies and television shows about the murders will undoubtedly be made in the future.

DIGGING FOR THE TRUTH AT THE DOZIER SCHOOL FOR BOYS

Marianna, Florida

The Florida State Reform School was established by an act of the legislature in 1897. It opened its doors on January 1, 1900. The school was administered by the governor and the cabinet of Florida. The name was changed to the Florida Industrial School for Boys in 1914 and to the Florida School for Boys in 1957. In 1967, the school was renamed in honor of a former superintendent, Arthur G. Dozier. A group of former students who called themselves "The White House Boys" after the building where they and others were "disciplined" with long leather straps participated in an investigation of the school in 2010, which found that the boys were routinely paddled and beaten. However, the investigation found no "physical evidence" supporting the stories that students were sexually assaulted. Nevertheless, the Arthur G. Dozier School was closed in 2011.

The story of the old reform school does not end with its closing. Approximately one hundred children died during their stay at the reform school. Many of them died in a dormitory fire in 1914 and in the flu epidemic of 1918. State records show that thirty-one former students were buried in the school cemetery. However, records also indicate that fifty other boys died there as well, but the site of their burial was not stated. A large number of the students who died there were impoverished African American boys who were probably buried in the "back side" of the reform school. Some people believe that the Ku Klux Klan "disposed of" the bodies of some of their victims in the cemetery. Rumors have circulated for years that another large gravesite exists somewhere on the former reform school's 1,400 acres. Some former students believe that the bodies of many of the students who died there were fed to the hogs.

In 2009, the governor's office instigated a state investigation of the burial sites at the former reform school as the result of newspaper articles published by the *Tampa Bay Times*. In its final report, the Florida Department of Law Enforcement's investigation accounted for thirty-one boys buried in the cemetery. Then in 2012, a research team from the University of Southern Florida used ground-penetrating radar to locate as many as nineteen more unmarked graves in the surrounding area, recovering teeth, bones and artifacts in each burial site. Led by anthropologist Erin Kimmerle, the team cleared the area and determined that at least forty-nine graves exist. The

197

investigation concluded that the school underreported deaths that occurred from blunt trauma and gunshot wounds. Kimmerle's team is helping the families of these boys achieve closure by comparing samples of their DNA with samples taken from the remains to determine who is buried there, as well as their ages and the circumstances of their deaths.

BIBLIOGRAPHY

Books

Asfar, Dan, and Edrick Thay. *Ghost Stories of the Civil War.* Edmonton AB, Canada: Ghost House Books, 2003.

Ball, Bonnie. *The Melungeons.* Johnson City, TN: Overmountain Press, 1997.

Blue and Gray Magazine's Guide to Haunted Places of the Civil War. Columbus, OH: Blue and Gray Magazine, 1996.

Brown, Alan. *Haunted Birmingham.* Charleston, SC: The History Press, 2008.

Brunvand, Jan Howard. *The Vanishing Hitchhiker: American Urban Legends and Their Meanings.* New York: W.W. Norton & Company, 1981.

Bunnell, James. *Strange Lights in West Texas.* Benbrook, TX: Lacey Publishing Company, 2009.

Carlson, Charlie. *Strange Florida: The Unexplained and Unusual.* New Smyrna Beach, FL: Luther Publishing, 1997.

Coleman, Christopher K. *Ghosts and Haunts of the Civil War.* Nashville, TN: Rutledge Hill Press, 1999.

Crain, Mary Beth. *Haunted U.S. Battlefields.* Guilford, CT: Globe Pequot Press, 2008.

Cunningham, Noble E., Jr. *In Pursuit of Reason: The Life of Thomas Jefferson.* Norwalk, CT: Easton Press, 1992.

Davis, Burke. *The Civil War: Strange & Fascinating Facts.* New York: Wings Books, 1982.

Floyd, E. Randall. *More Great Southern Mysteries.* New York: Barnes & Noble Books, 1990.

Fort, Charles. *The Book of the Damned.* New York: Ace Books, 1972.

Hillhouse, Larry. *Ghosts of Lookout Mountain.* Weaver, IA: Quixote Press, 2017.

Kennedy, Francis H., ed. *The Civil War Battlefield Guide.* Boston: Houghton Mifflin, 1990.

Kennedy, N. Brent. *The Melungeons: The Resurrection of a Proud People; An Untold Story of Ethnic Cleansing in America.* Macon, GA: Mercer University Press, 1997.

Kermeen, Frances. *Ghostly Encounters: True Stories of America's Haunted Inns and Hotels.* New York: Warner Books, 2002.

Kotarski, Georgiana. *Ghosts of the Southern Tennessee Valley*. Winston-Salem, NC: John F. Blair Publisher, 2006.

Long, Carolyn Morrow. *A New Orleans Voudou Priestess: The Legend and Reality of Marie Laveau*. Gainesville: University Press of Florida, 2006.

Mapp, Alf J., Jr. *Thomas Jefferson: Passionate Pilgrim*. Lanham, MD: Rowman and Littlefield Publishers, 2009.

Moore, Dot. *Oracle of the Ages*: *Reflections on the Curious Life of Fortune Teller Mayhayley Lancaster*. Montgomery, AL: New South Books, 2001.

Penot, Jessica, and Amy Petulla. *Haunted Chattanooga*. Charleston, SC: The History Press, 2011.

Robertson, William G. *The Battle of Chickamauga*. Fort Washington, PA: Eastern National, 1995.

Satterfield, Carolyn Green. *Historic Sites of Jefferson County, Alabama*. Birmingham, AL: Jefferson County Historical Commission, 1976.

Schaefer, Susan. *The Crescent Hotel with Ghost Stories*. Springfield, MO: self-published, 2017.

Scott, Norman, and Beth Scott. *Haunted America*. New York: Tor, 1994.

Tallant, Robert. *Voodoo in New Orleans*. New York: MacMillan, 1974.

Taylor, Troy. *Beyond the Grave*. Alton, IL: Whitechapel Press, 2001.

———. *The Haunting of America*. Alton, IL: Whitechapel Press, 2001.

Walser, Richard. *North Carolina Legends*. Raleigh: North Carolina Office of Archives and History, 1980.

Wilson, Patty A. *Cursed in the Carolinas: Stories of the Damned*. Guilford, CT: Globe Pequot, 2017.

Windham, Kathryn. *Alabama*: *One Big Front Porch*. Tuscaloosa: University of Alabama Press, 1974.

———. *Jeffrey Introduces 13 More Southern Ghosts*. Huntsville, AL: Strode Publishers, 1971.

———. *Jeffrey's Latest 13*. Tuscaloosa: University of Alabama Press, 1982.

———. *13 Alabama Ghosts and Jeffrey*. Tuscaloosa: University of Alabama Press, 1969.

———. *13 Mississippi Ghosts and Jeffrey*. Tuscaloosa: University of Alabama Press, 2015.

———. *13 Tennessee Ghosts and Jeffrey*. Tuscaloosa: University of Alabama Press, 1977.

Articles

Abandoned Country. "The Church Hill Tunnel; Two Portals a World Apart." www.abandonedcountry.com.

Abandoned Florida. "Arthur G. Dozier School for Boys." www.abandonedfl.com.

About North Georgia. "Battle Above the Clouds." www.aboutnorthgeorgia.com.

Alan's Mysterious World. "Captain Tony's Haunted Saloon." alansmysteriousworld.wordpress.com.

AL.com. "Alabama's 60,000-Year-Old Underwater Forest Spills Its Secrets in New Documentary." www.al.com.

All Smoky Mountain Vacations. "History of the Cherokee Indians." www.allsomkymountainvacations.com.

American Battlefield Trust. "Battle of Fredericksburg." www.battlefields.org.
————. "Battle of Lookout Mountain—November 24, 1863." www.battlefields.org.
————. "John Clem." www.battlefields.org.
American Ghost Stories. "Third Eye Man—Columbia, SC." americanghoststories.com.
AmusingPlanet. "A Hanging Tree, Graves and Hemingway: The Colorful History of Captain Tony's Saloon." www.amusingplanet.com.
Ancient Lost Treasures. "Hampton House Buried Treasure." www.ancientlosttreasures.com.
And Speaking of Which. "Stuckey's Bridge." andspeakingofwhich.blogspot.com.
Anomalies, the Strange & Unexpected. "1835, January 5: Mr. H's Odd Wound." anomalyinfo.com.
Appalachian History. "The (Accidental) Discovery of a Lifetime." www.appalachianhistory.net.
————. "The Brown Mountain Lights." www.appalachianhistory.net.
Atlas Obscura. "Church Hill Tunnel." www.atlasobscura.com.
————. "The Devil's Millhopper." www.atlasobscura.com.
————. "Georgia Guidestones." www.atlasobscura.com.
————. "Grave of the Lady in Red." www.atlasobscura.com.
————. "Grave of Stonewall Jackson's Arm." www.atlasobscura.com.
————. "Pope Lick Trestle Bridge." www.atlasobscura.com
————. "Skunk Ape Research Headquarters." www.atlasobscura.com.
————. "The Witch of Pungo Statue." www.atlasobscura.com.
Barefoot, Daniel. "Devil's Horse's Hoof Prints." ncpedia.org.
BBC. "The truth about a strange blood-sucking monster." www.bbc.com.
Beale Treasure Story. "Beale Treasure Story." www.bealetreasurestory.com.
Biography. "Nostradamus." www.biography.com.
Bustle. "What Are the Texas Killing Fields? This Mystery Will Keep You Up at Night." www.bustle.com.
Can You Actually. "The Haunted Church Hill Tunnel Has a Horrifically Creepy Backstory." canyouactually.com.
Causey, Donna R. "A Civil War Romance in Ensley, Alabama Has Two Heroines—Which Is Correct?" Alabama Pioneers. www.alabamapioneers.com.
————. "Have You Ever Seen This Face in the Courthouse Window in Pickens County, Alabama?" Alabama Pioneers. alabamapioneers.com
CBS Dallas/Fort Worth. "Did John Wilkes Booth Hide Out in Granbury?" dfw.cbslocal.com.
CBS News. "The Real-Life Mystery of Texas' Killing Fields." cbsnews.com.
The Christian Post. "Lesson Learned from N.C.'s 'The Devil's Tramping Ground' and Providence Church." www.christianpost.com.
Citizen Times. "Melungeons Explore Mysterious Mixed-Race Origins." www.citizen-times.com.
City of Aurora, Texas. "Ned—The Aurora Alien." www.auroratexas.gov.
City of Bishopville. "Bishopville, South Carolina." cityofbishopvillesc.com.
Civil War Roundtable. "The Search for Lost Confederate Gold." clevelandcivilwarroundtable.com.
CNN. "Case of the Missing Heiress: Who Killed Jacqueline Levitz?" www.edition.cnn.com.
————. "Florida to Exhume Bodies Buried at Former Boys School." www.cnn.com.

Crescent Hotel. "Bizarre Discovery at a Eureka Springs (AR) Mountaintop Spa Resport Reads Like a Chilling Novel." Crescent-hotel.com.

The Crux. "Georgia's Own Doomsday Stonehenge Monument." blogs. discovermagaine.com.

Cryptidz. "Grunch Road Monster." cryptidz.wikia.com.

———. "Lake Herrington Monster." cryptidz.wikia.com.

Cryptopia. "Devil Monkeys: (North America)." cryptopia.us

Cryptoville. "What Is a Rougarou, Exactly?" visitcryptoville.com.

Curren, Caleb, and Steve Newby. "The Mystery of the Alabama Stone Site." *PAL Journal.* January 2018.

Daily Gamecock. "The Legend of the Third Eye Man." www.dailygamecock.com.

Destination Strange. "Mistress Marie Laveau: The Real Story of the Voodoo Queen of New Orleans." roadtrippers.com.

Dickson, Gordon. "Reward Offered for Return of Stolen UFO Alien Grave Marker in Texas." *Fort Worth Star-Telegram*, March 30, 2018.

Discover South Carolina. "Beware the Lizard Man!" discoversouthcarolina.com.

Dreaming Casually. "The True Legend of Julia Legare—Face vs. Fiction." dreamingcasuallypoetry.blogspot.com.

Eckhardt, C.F. "Did John Wilkes Booth Live in Texas?" Texas Escapes. www. texasescapes.com.

Edisto Beach. "The Legend of Julia Legare." www.edistobeach.com.

Encyclopedia of Arkansas. "Fouke Monster." www.encyclopediaofarkansas.net.

———. "Petit Jean Mountain [Legend]." www.encyclopediaofarkansas.net.

Encyclopedia of Virginia. "Grace Sherwood (ca. 1660–1740)." www. enclopediavirginia.org.

Exemplore. "The Bunny Man: Evolution of a Legend." exemplore.com.

———. "The Grunch: A Chupacabra on the Bayou." exemplore.com.

———. "The Rougarou: Louisiana's Cajun Werewolf." exemplore.com.

Explore Edisto. "Buried Alive on Edisto Island." www.exploreedisto.com.

"The Faithful Vigil of 'Floating Island.'" *Port of Mobile* (August 1983): 21–25.

Family Tree. "The Mystery of the Melungeons." www.familytreemagazine.com.

Fitzhugh, Pat. "The Bell Witch Haunting." The Bell Witch. www.bellwitch.org.

Flagler Museum. "Henry Morrison Flagler Biography." flaglermuseum.us.

Florida State Parks. "History of Devil's Millhopper." www.floridastateparks.org.

Fox News. "Texas Woman Claims to Have Found Mythical 'Chucupacabra.'" foxnews.com.

Fredericksburg.com. "The Angel of Marye's Heights." fredericksburg.com.

Galveston Ghost. "The Face of UTMB—Haunted Galveston Island, Texas." www. galvestonghost.com.

Gannon, Megan. "7,000-Year-Old Native American Burial Site Found Underwater." National Geographic. news.nationalgeographic.com.

Geocaching. "The Lost Shults Mine." www.geocaching.com.

Geocities. "The Chesapeake Bay Sea Monster." www.goecities.com.

Ghost Stories. "Three-Legged Lady Road." paranormalstories.blogspot.com.

The Guardian. "Robert Johnson Sells His Soul to the Devil." www.theguardian.com.

Hancock County Historical Society. "The James Copeland Gang." www. hancockcountyhistoricalsociety.com.

Heartland Cabin Rentals. "Campfire Stories: The Lost Gold Mine." www. heartlandrentals.com.

Historical Marker Database. "Mystery Shrouds Fort Morgan." www.hmdb.org.

Historic Mysteries. "What Happened to Bobby Dunbar?" www.historicmysteries.com.

History. "Civil War Technology." www.history.com.

———. "The Goliad Massacre—The Other Alamo." www.history.com.

HistoryNet. "The Confederate Floating Battery Revival during the American Civil War." historynet.com.

Hometown Forums. "Old Mystery Cleared Up…Or Is It??" www.hometownforums.com.

Huffington Post. "Oldest Bar Is an Ex-Morgue with Bodies Still Buried in It." www.huffpost.com.

Internet Sacred Text Archive. "Siren of the French Broad." www.sacred-texts.com.

Kazek, Kelly. "A Look at Bryce hospital, Alabama's Historic Insane Asylum, Then and Now." www.al.com.

———. "The Truth behind 9 Urban Legends about Auburn and Alabama." www.al.com.

Keene, Pamela A. "How the Dead Brought New Life to Senoia." *Georgia Magazine* (September 2017): 18–22.

Legends & Rumors. "Nostradamus Predicted Halloween Campus Massacre." legendsrumors.blogspot.com.

Legends of America. "Confederate Gold in Wilkes County, Georgia." www.legendsofamerica.com.

———. "The Haunted Crescent Hotel in Eureka Springs." www.legendsofamerica.com.

———. "Legends of Fort Mountain, Georgia." www.legendsofamerica.com.

———. "Witch Dance of the Natchez Trace." www.legendofamerica.com.

Live Science. "What Are the Marfa Lights? www.livescience.com.

Local Lore and Gore. "The World's Most Famous Melungeon?" localloreandgore.com.

Medical Bag. "Dozier School: Campus of Death." www.medicalbag.com

Mississippi Encyclopedia. "James Copeland." mississippiencyclopedia.org.

MNN Coast. "Underwater Forest Is an Ancient 'Fairy World' Found Just Off the Alabama Coast." www.mnn.com.

Mostly Ghosts. "Hell's Gate in Alabama." http://mostlyghosts.com.

Mutual UFO Network. "Pascagoula Mississippi Case." www.mufon.com.

Mysterious Universe. "The Betz Mystery Sphere: Alien Artifact or Doomsday Device?" mysteriousuniverse.org.

———. "North Carolina's New Mystery Island Retreats Back into the Sea." mysteriousuniverse.org.

MythBusters Results. "MythBusters Episode 40: Confederate Rocket." mythresults.com.

NBC 5 Dallas-Fort Worth. "Mystery Still Engulfs Lake Worth Monster." www.nbcdfw.com.

NCPedia. "Devil's Tramping Ground." www.christianpost.com.

New Georgia Encyclopedia. "Confederate Gold." www.georigiaencyclopedia.org.

Nickell, Joe. "The Brown Mountain Lights: Solved!" *Skeptical Inquirer*, vol. 40 (January/February 2016).

North Carolina Ghost Stories. "The Siren of the French Broad." northcarolinghosts.com.

NPR. "The Curious Fate of Stonewall Jackson's Arm." www.npr.org.

Ohio History Central. "Johnny Klem." www.ohiohistorycentral.org.

P. Allen Smith. "Halloween Haunts in Arkansas." pallensmith.com.

Paranormal Encounters. "Legend Tripping—What Is It?" www.paranormal-encounters.com.

Paranormal Investigating. "Mayhayley Lancaster: Seer, Psychic, and So Much More." paranormalinvestigating.com.

Paranormal Society. "Hell's Gate Bridge." oxfordparanormalsociety.com.

Pelican State of Mind. "History of the Rougarou." pelicanstateofmind.com.

Pine Barrens Institute. "Cryptid Profile: The Herrington Lake Ell-Pig." www.pinebarrensinstitute.com.

Prairie Ghosts. "The Gurdon Light: Clark County, Arkansas." www.prairieghosts.com.

Raccoon Mountain. "Raccoon Mountain Caverns & Campground." www.raccoonmountain.com.

Ranker. "The Pope Lick Monster Is No Mere Urban Legend—He Has an Actual Body Count." www.ranker.com.

———. "The Terrifying True Story of the Bunnyman, North Virginia's Most Gruesome Urban Legend." www.ranker.com.

Receipt Book of Carolina Dean. "Mary Ingleman: The First Witch of Winnsboro South Carolina." receipt-book-blogspot.com.

Reelfoot Lake, Tennessee. "Reelfoot Lake." reelfoottourism.com.

Rennie, Daniel. "The Mysterious Disappearance of Aaron Burr's Daughter." allthatsinteresting.com.

Revo Revolvy. "Boyington Oak." www.revolving.com.

Roadside America. "Graves of the King and Queen of the Gypsies." www.roadsideamerica.com.

———. "Kelly, Kentucky: Little Green Men Festival." roadsideamerica.com.

S8nt.com. "Chesapeake Bay Sea Monster?" www.s8int.com.

Scientific American. "The Great Kentucky Meat Shower Mystery Unwound by Projectile Vulture Vomit." blogs.scientificamerican.com.

The Signal. "'Lady in Black' Haunts Henderson Campus." www.obusignal.com.

Sirenian. "The Chessie Watch Page." www.sirenian.org.

Skeptic Files. "The Following Interview Took Place on Wednesday, 4 November, in Wytheville, VA." www.skepticfiles.org.

Smith, Phillip. "Aboriginal Constructions in the Southern Piedmont." University of Georgia Laboratory of Archaeology Series, Report No. 4, 1962.

Smithsonian. "Archaeologists Finally Know What Happened at This Brutal Reform School." www.smithsonianmag.com.

———. "On the Trail of Florida's Bigfoot—the Skunk Ape." www.smithsonianmag.com

Smithsonian Institution Archives. "The St. Augustine Monster." siarchives.si.edu.

Smithsonian National Postal Museum. "Legend of the Singing River." postalmuseum.si.edu.

Smoky Mountain Navigator. "History of Gatlinburg, Tennessee." www.smokymountainnavigator.com.

South Carolina Plantations. "Hampton Plantation—McClellanville—Charleston County." south-carolina-plantations.com.

South Carolina Public Radio News and Talk. "30 Years Later, the Legend of the Lizard Man Lives On in Bishopville." scpublicradio.org.

Supernatural Magazine. "The Brown Mountain Lights Mystery: What Are They?" supernaturalmagazine.com.

Texas Escapes. "The Cart War Oak: Goliad Hanging Tree." www.texasescapes.com.

Texas Forest Service. "Cart War Oak." texasforestservice.tamu.edu.

Texas UFO Museum & Research Library. "Huffman 1980." roswellbooks.com.

Thoughtco. "1955: The Kelly, Kentucky, Alien Invasion." www.thoughtco.com.

Tuscaloosa Area Virtual Museum. "University of Alabama Cemetery, 1960." Tavm.omeka.net.

Unexplained America. "Mysterious Falls from the Sky: It's Raining Fish & Frogs!" www.prairieghosts.com/falls_sky.htm.

Unknown Explorers. "Devil Monkeys." www.unknownexplorers.com.

Unresolved Mysteries. "Where Is Jacqueline Levitz?" www.reddit.com.

Unsolvedmysteries.wikia.com. "Wytheville UFO Sightings." http://unsolvedmysteries.wikia.com.

UVA Magazine. "Ghoulish Grounds: Hair-Raising Tales from around the University." http://uvamagaine.org/articles/ghoulish_grounds.

Vintage News. "The Mystery of Bobby Dunbar's Disappearance." www.thevintagenews.com.

Wbir.com. "Appalachian Unsolved: Dennis Martin, Missing in the Smokies." www.wbir.com.

Wdam.com. "Know Where You Go: Is There Hidden Gold in Perry County?" www.wdam.com.

Women of Every Complexion and Complexity. "The Lady and the Patriot: Theodosia Burr's Fateful Voyage." womenofeverycomplexionandcomplexity.weebly.com.

Your Ghost Stories. "The Crescent Hotel." www.yourghoststories.com.

Newspapers

Aumick, Amy. "Devil's Millhopper, the Most Interesting Hole in Florida." *Orlando Sentinel*, May 14, 2017.

Bowers, Larry. "Tales of a Cherokee 'Tall Betsy?'" *Cleveland Daily Banner*, October 28, 2015.

Broom, Brian. "'No One to Pray Over Her': Unearthed in 1969, Lady in Red Remains a Mystery." *Clarion Ledger*, February 17, 2019.

Brown, Robbie. "A Georgia Main Street Paved in Red Carpet." *New York Times*, December 2, 2012.

Goodwin, Juliana. "Relive a Haunted History on the Ghostly Grounds of the Crescent Hotel." *News-Leader*, October 13, 2016.

Huntsville Times. "NASA Marks 50th Anniversary of Monkeys Able and Miss Baker in Space." May 28, 2009.

Jacobs, Jennifer. "The Hanging Man at Stuckey's Bridge." *Meridian Star*, October 28, 2007.

———. "Queen Kelly Mitchell: A Slice of Meridian's History." *Meridian Star*, December 25, 2007.

Kokomo (IN) Tribune. "Ghosts or Gasses? Tree Cries, Crowds Listen." May 1, 1987.

Leonard, Pat. "The Angel of Marye's Heights." *New York Times*, December 14, 2012.

Price, Mark. "Thinking of Visiting NC's Mysterious Shelly Island for Spring Break? Think Again." *Charlotte Observer*, March 9, 2018.

Reeder, Carolyn. "Drummer Boys Played Important Roles in the Civil War, and Some Became Soldiers." *Washington Post*, February 21, 2012.

Shu, Alissa. "Mystery of Hazlehurst: Boy Warned of Tornado." *Clarion Ledger*, January 23, 2019.

Tyler, Zach. "Oxford's Long-Closed Hell's Gate Bridge Has Uncertain Future." *Aniston Star,* January 18, 2017.

Warren, Beth. "Pope Lick 'Monster' Survivor 'Mentally Crushed.'" *Courier Journal,* March 6, 2016.

Windham, Ben. "The Mystery of the Rattlesnake Disc." *Tuscaloosa News,* February 12, 2006.

ABOUT THE AUTHOR

Alan Brown was born in Alton, Illinois, on January 12, 1950. After earning degrees from Millikin University, Southern Illinois University, Illinois State University and the University of Illinois, he taught high school English in Flora and Springfield, Illinois. In 1986, he joined the English faculty at the University of West Alabama. When he is not teaching, Alan enjoys watching old movies, traveling with his wife, Marilyn, and spending time with his grandsons, Cade and Owen. Since publishing his first book, *Dim Roads and Dark Nights*, in 1993, he has explored his interest in folklore, especially ghost tales, in over thirty publications, including *Stories from the Haunted South* (2004), *Haunted Georgia* (2006), *Ghost Hunters of the South* (2006), *Ghost Hunters of New England* (2008), *Haunted Birmingham* (2009), *The Big Book of Texas Ghost Stories* (2010), *Haunted Meridian* (2011), *Ghosts along the Mississippi River* (2012), *Ghosts of Florida's Gulf Coast* (2014), *The Haunted South* (2014), *Ghosts of Mississippi's Golden Triangle* (2016), *The Haunted Southwest* (2016), *The Haunting of Alabama* (2017) and *Eerie Alabama* (2019).

Visit us at
www.historypress.com